Nonstandardized Quests

NONSTANDARDIZED QUESTS

500+
Writing
Prompts
That
Matter

DAVID E. LeCOUNT

Foreword by
Susan Ohanian

HEINEMANN
PORTSMOUTH, NH

Heinemann
A division of Reed Elsevier Inc.
361 Hanover Street
Portsmouth, NH 03801–3912
www.heinemann.com

Offices and agents throughout the world

Library of Congress Cataloging-in-Publication Data
LeCount, David E.
    Nonstandardized quests : 500+ writing prompts that matter /
David E. LeCount.
        p. cm.
    ISBN 0-86709-522-9 (alk. paper)
    1. English language—Composition and exercises—Study and teaching.
2. Language arts. I. Title.

LB1576 .L375 2002
808'.042'071—dc21   2001051684

Editor: Lois Bridges
Production: Lynne Reed
Typesetter: Drawing Board Studios
Cover design: Lisa Fowler
Manufacturing: Steve Bernier

Printed in the United States of America on acid free paper
06   05   04   03   02   DA   1   2   3   4   5

This book is dedicated to my family, all of them—
My mother, father, and sisters; wife Arla and sons Jason,
Joshua, and Daniel, the ones who share my absence as I write;
and the ones who write or call to give me ongoing help and support:
Lois Bridges, Jim and Pat Hackett, Herb Kohl, Naomi
Lee, Mara Mills, Susan Ohanian, Denette Sauré, Kuangkai and
Estella Tai, and the youngest, Christopher Tai.
To my brother Tom, who died too soon.

FOREWORD
Susan Ohanian

In 1973, a *New York Times* reporter noted that Edward Gorey had attended every performance of the New York City Ballet for seventeen years. Noting that the New York City Ballet was the best, Gory admitted, "You can often hear me bitching about somebody's performance, but I'm bitching on a terribly high level." Still, asked a writer for *Dance Magazine*, "Tell me how anyone can sit through thirty-nine Nutcrackers in one season." Gorey replied, "At first I thought, my God, this is the most boring ballet in the history of the world. Then I began to go more and more." Then Gorey added, "Naturally, one of the reasons for going to Nutcracker is to watch the mice carry on—somebody's doing something crazy and new and different every night . . ."

What an image. Attending all those ballet performances. What an image. Correcting all those English themes. Year after year after year. The reality is that our mice are much more likely to offer something crazy and new and different if the prompts we offer are also crazy and new and different. Yes, even with the quirky, provocative, quite wonderful prompts of *Nonstandardized Quests: 500+ Writing Prompts That Matter*, English teachers will still be bitching about somebody's performance but these prompts will get everybody bitching on a terribly high level.

As someone who writes for a living, I love prompts. I can't think of a book I've written that wasn't inspired by the phone call from an editor offering those magic words, "Can you write an article on . . . ?" Of course I said yes. Every time. A definition of a writer too often ignored is: Writing when you don't want to. I wrote "Insults to the Soul" for *English Journal* because Leila Christenbury asked me to do it. I admired her nerve—asking for an article she knew would be critical of NCTE policy on standards. So far, four books have come from Leila's prompt. After the third one I thought, finished at last. No more to say. Then the phone rang.

Years ago, when I served on a committee to create prompts for the state's first writing test, someone suggested, "Describe your favorite teacher." I objected, insisting that "tell how you and your classmates annoy a teacher you don't like" was much more likely to elicit strong writing. State ed functionaries were horrified. No negativism allowed. Since, more often than not, my writing is enlivened by things that annoy me, I find such an imperative alarming as well as nutty. Now the prescription for pleasantries reigns supreme, making the chestnut "How did you spend your summer vacation?" seem almost audacious. Here is one set of prompts from one state exam:

Kindergarten: Think about a time of year you really like . . .

Grade 4: Think about a time of year you really like . . .

Grade 9: Think about a time of year you really like . . .

There you have it: the one-size-fits-all universal flat-as-a-bureaucrat's-soul prompt. One year "Describe a favorite person" sweeps the country; another year it's "Describe a favorite meal."

Youth of America, try to stay awake.

Reading "exemplary responses" to pallid prompts on high stakes tests convinces me that following state writing directives produces Stepford children. I was in the midst of reading these robotic responses when my email pal David LeCount sent some of his "nonstandard" writing prompts. I was electrified. There is something here to offend everyone, and this is important. David, English teacher, award-winning haiku poet, bush pilot, gentleman goose farmer, helps students see that to write anything more than a job application form is to take risks.

While playing around with David's prompts I ended up at the Batesville Casket Company Internet site, as well as the Body Farm in Tennessee. I learned about Indian sign language, virtual pet cemeteries, a cyclotron analysis of the Gutenberg Bible, the protection and conservation of southwest native trout, the Alaska Native Language Center, mule sterility, Napier's logarithm, the derivation of a famous four-letter word, and hundreds more.

David brings to *Nonstandardized Quests: 500+ Writing Prompts That Matter* two important principles: Write about what you know. Write about what you don't know. The first constrains most people. The second demonstrates how writers stand on the shoulders of other writers; it offers a world limited only by the writer's imagination.

INTRODUCTION

I was lucky enough to grow up in a family that delighted in words. Though I did not realize it at the time, the phrases and words that I heard as a child carved my life before me.

As I sat at the dinner table, I heard the phrase at dessert-time "Don't take more than your share!" I heard "That isn't fair," usually from a brother or sister. In the larger adult world, I heard "Stop taking sides," usually from elders admonishing one or the other. But what I enjoy most, as I look back, is my father's answer for everything we did, usually spontaneously. We asked, "Why?" and his indelible answer was, "Just for the fun of it." I have not heard such a beautiful phrase since.

Such phrases were not only in English. Sometimes they were in Spanish or French or German. Because my parents were divorced, I was enriched by strange languages in different homes. The love of sounds was also conveyed by my mother's love of Shakespeare and Frost, and my father's love of Louis Armstrong and Edvard Grieg. And above all and perhaps better than all, words from *The Big Sky* by A. B. Guthrie read around a campfire in the Wind River Mountains of Wyoming, where the shadows of a moose passed across our tent.

For me language became unbounded music. It is nothing less than a means by which to discover the world. It is fingers probing the darkness like a tarantula.

At the same time that I fell in love with words, I entered school and became vaguely aware that words lacked the enchantment I had felt at home and often turned the discovery of meaning into drudgery, the song of words into the singsong of competition for grades. For about six years I mostly gave up on my love of words and worked for grades, a betrayal I am not proud to say I was fairly good at.

Later, in college, I learned that I might have both so long as I didn't take homework or schooling too seriously and allowed myself plenty of time to write. In this seditious activity, some professors helped me—in fact, helped me immeasurably.

During this period of several years, I began to formulate what was to become my philosophy for teaching creative writing and writing in general. The principles were simple and few. The questions or prompts that I would ask would not require a five-paragraph essay. I had to give creative questions in order to get creative responses. The prompts needed to be multidisciplinary so as to reach everyone's interests and strengths and cultures. Answers had to surprise me, had to be something I hadn't expected. Humor had to be possible. There had to be no "right" answer. Feathers had to be ruffled. Quite simply put, trite questions required/inspired trite responses. The same kind of stuff that had verbally castrated me when I was in high school.

Armed with this philosophy, I walked into a classroom in 1969 as a substitute and was disheartened by what I saw. Children who were beaten at home by parents were asked to describe what they did on their summer vacation. It was the gap in classes and subject matter that troubled me the most. My fourth-year Latin class, it was suddenly clear, in a nearly all-black school had only white kids in it. Belatedly, I remembered the words of my mother from my childhood: "The law punishes the rich and poor alike for stealing a crust of bread."

Nonetheless, I soon found and settled into a teaching position in a wealthy community north of what was to become Silicon Valley. For twenty years I taught everything from Advanced Placement English to Fundamental Composition. However, increasingly I felt I was compromising on what I believed in. Students needed to get a four or a five on the AP Exam. Parents needed their children to get into Harvard or Princeton, needed more homework, needed better grades, needed better SAT scores, and the catch-all, more "rigor." In their journals students reflected their own depression and doubts that they would ever "live up" to the expectations. Not a single child knew when his efforts were good enough to achieve love or success. I looked about me and found that most colleagues were frightened by the economically powerful parents. Some wanted to buddy up to the parents, some helped students write papers, and many kept silent. In this school, the affluent parents got their children into the "right" classes. Some parents went so far as to write their child's application to a college the student didn't even want to go to. No one wanted to rock the boat.

The turning point came in 1989 when I had been a presenter for the California Association of Teachers of English in Los Angeles. My presentation was evaluated by many fellow teachers (K–12+), as is the practice, and fifty-four out of fifty-five rated me as "excellent." Naturally, this kind of affirmation went to my head and I was delighted. It reinforced my feeling that I did not need to heed the parents who were obsessed with competition and lacked delight. Yet, when I returned to campus, I met a colleague in the hallway who cursorily suggested that my class needed more "rigor," more writing. That comment at just the right time was enough to turn my simmering dissatisfaction into action. It was enough to make me request a change of schools.

But that was not easy for me to do after teaching twenty years at the same school. A few "friends" ridiculed my decision to leave. All the same, I looked throughout the district for a school I wanted to move to. The one that appealed to me most was the most socio-economically underprivileged in the district. I worried I might fail in an environment where students weren't already ready to go. There was no protocol for the interview between me and the instructional vice principal and the English department head. Quite frankly, they said, no one had ever made such a switch. Nevertheless I did it.

I

At my new school, I learned a different kind of teaching. I had to relate differently to the kids, and they to me. I had to revive my Spanish. Students trusted me with problems I found difficult to believe: living without their own parents, working too many hours to do their homework, being molested or raped, dealing with parents who were alcoholics or drug addicts, mourning friends lost to gang fights. They had trouble learning in class because they had higher priorities. Parents were working two jobs and so they had to baby-sit a younger sibling. Their cars were in the shop and they couldn't get to school. An uncle had died and they had a funeral to attend. Most disturbing of all was that the students did not believe in their minds, they had been so beaten down emotionally.

What they had in common with my other school was that they were depressed. No one knew how to play as a child. No one knew when enough was enough. I think of it now as the competitive hop-scotch syndrome. A corruption of the protected games of childhood with the brutal competition of adulthood in America.

What they didn't have in common with my former school is that they didn't keep their parents' secrets. In the upper-class school students were largely secretive of molestation, cocaine addictions, and infidelities. What I believe in retrospect is that they were expected to be loyal members of the family and in turn they would get the privileges of going to big-name universities, BMWs, and keys to the good life. In other words, they were expected to keep quiet. In spite of this, some students broke the code. And I learned of adulteries, drug addictions, broken families, and economic woes.

II

With this background, I began to write assignments that I thought would appeal to "children" as they really were: full of superficial adulthood and responsibilities, sex and expectations, stress and traumas. But completely lacking in the deep-down sense of play, just for the fun of it. Assignments that I believed might heal and restore the sense of joy for the sake of joy, love of words for the love of words.

In many ways, I failed. Students did not trust me because I was an adult, and part of the system. And they viewed me as an impediment to getting into the "right" school. Many, I believe, wished I would get serious (and more serious) and teach how to jump better through the hoops.

In some other ways, I succeeded with remarkable responses and affection. Students with "high expectations" were glad to be relieved of duty. And some students with "low expectations" were glad to see some part of school as fun. When I exercised the play of my imagination, they responded in kind, and in kindness. I encouraged humor and believe that humor took much of the stress out of their lives.

I include the following as Exhibit A to show how creative questions can provoke creative responses.

One-Line Creative Quiz Responses

1. Question: Why aren't portholes square?
   Student response: "Because squares excite whales."
2. Question: What does a pickle relish?
   Student response: "The thought of a cute cumber."
3. Question: Whose national anthem is "home on the range"?
   Student response: "Ma and Pa Kettles."
4. Question: What was the regiment of armed cactuses created for?
   Student responses: "To separate the prickly pairs," and "Arming petunias would be pointless."
5. Question: What determines the number of leaves on a four-leaf clover?
   Student responses: "A three leaf clover," and "Counting."

I found that at both schools, these students who seemed to have so little in common shared untapped reserves of imagination, joy, and hope.

NOTE TO READERS

In the appendix, you will find a list of websites that coincide with many of the prompts. Share these with your students as a way to invite additional research and learning—and, of course, to promote the joy of nonstandardized quests!

SIMPLY WRITE:

(Let your students know which topics require more research than others.)

1. A letter to your grandmother for her birthday that demonstrates an understanding of Mexican American culture.

2. A letter to the parent who was not given custody after your parents were divorced.

3. A transcript of your evidentiary testimony involving the witnessing of a serious crime.

4. An encyclopedia entry that describes the fall of the Alamo from the Mexican point of view.

5. A written transcript of at least *five* 911 phone calls that depict an ongoing instance of spousal abuse.

6. A brief (100-word) prayer that a slave who lived in Georgia during the Civil War might give. (Near Andersonville, 1863)

7. An FBI report on the friends, activities, and opinions of your favorite sports hero.

8. A day's diet for the world's heaviest person who wants to be a lot thinner soon. (It needs to take basic nourishment needs into consideration.)

9. A movie review that criticizes three scenes— including the specific dialogue—because of sexism.

10. A song that celebrates the winning of the Battle of the Little Big Horn from the point of view of the Lakota Sioux.

11. A survival manual for young trout, who are often sought by fly fishermen.

12. A decision by the Supreme Court that explains why it will require all students to wear uniforms in public schools.

13. A pamphlet by a coalition of African Americans and Mexican Americans that lists and explains their reasons for calling for a new Constitutional Convention.

14. A sonnet written by a chemistry professor.

Chemistry Poem
BY LIZZIE CORRY

Hi, I'm Mr. Mabel
We don't learn out of a book
By heart, we know the periodic table
Step inside and take a look

My favorite element is copper
Their favorite is zinc
It is a chart topper
Just like my wife's mink

Kids here, Kids there
They don't listen to anything
There are bottles and beakers everywhere
The kids just want the bell to ring

Chemistry is a blast
From the present to the past

15. A thank-you note to the French from the president for the gift of the Statue of Liberty.

16. The last will and testament of Charles Darwin, explaining to his heirs who gets what and why.

17. A tourist's guide to Puritan New England during the Salem witchcraft trials.

18. A barnyard animal's guide to surviving the humiliations and goals of 4-H.

19. An Alcoholics Anonymous father's advice to his son who has just received his driver's license.

20. A dialogue/fight between a mother and a father over who spends the most money.

21. The advice of a Mexican American patriarch to his sons on how to survive the violence of the ghetto.

22. The advice of a child to his/her teddy bear on how to survive another night of asthma.

23. A mother's advice to her daughter on how to deal with sexual harassment at her workplace.

24. A doctor's notes on how to create the perfect health plan for all the people of America.

25. A ten-item list of the calls a blue jay might make and what they mean.

26. A ten-item list of an Eskimo's favorite movies.

27. A young cat's training manual—given by her mother—on ten ways to train human beings.

A Young Cat's Training Manual

BY SALVADOR JARA

1. Meow when you want food.

2. If that doesn't work, crawl around their legs.

3. Always sit in the places that they are about to sit in to show them who's boss.

4. Claw on the door whenever you want it opened.

5. Leave your food uneaten to show the human which foods you like and which you do not. This might take a while but the human will eventually learn.

6. Whenever you move into a new house, make sure to urinate everywhere to make sure your human knows where your territory lies.

7. If you don't want him or her to wear a certain article of clothing, go sit on the clothes. And leave some of your fur on it. They'll get the point and not wear it.

8. Lie in the center of the bed to make them sleep around you. I was told it's good for their back from a smart alley cat.

9. Drink from the toilet whenever the humans aren't treating you right. They'll run to get you and take you over to fresh, clean water.

10. Whenever you want to get a laugh out of them, just do one of your many talents.

28. A guide to calling by phone your parent with Alzheimer's disease.

29. A visitors guide to etiquette in the veterans ward of a mental hospital.

30. An immigrant's guide on how to sleep in small quarters.

31. The public statement to the press of a man convicted of stealing ten billion dollars of the public's money.

32. A note of explanation from a four-star general to a congressional committee as to why Americans were tested for the effects of radiation in the 1950s.

33. A letter from the physicist to the emperor of Japan on "Why I invented the atomic bomb."

34. A conversation between a mother and her daughter on "Why your father and I got a divorce."

35. A pro-life minister's last sermon before he commits suicide.

36. An AIDS patient's last words to his son.

37. A ten-item menu for a Mexican Chinese restaurant.

ChinaMex

BY DONALD GOMEZ

ChinaMex
Open all day every day 24/7

1. Beijing Burrito $4.50
   Your choice of chicken, beef, or pork with rice, beans, sour cream, onions, a zesty salsa roja, and either sweet and sour or soy sauce.

2. Chihuahua Chow Mein $4.00
   This spicy little number is always a crowd-pleaser with its hearty noodles and homemade hot sauce draped with mouth-watering pieces of either beef or chicken, and topped with sliced avocado squares or guacamole.

3. Manchurian Nachos $4.50
   Authentic Chinese potstickers smothered in our 1-of-a-kind nacho cheese sauce. Add red or green salsa at no extra charge.

4. El Paso Fried Rice $5.00
   A generous portion of long grain Spanish rice tossed with roast pork or duck and sautéed onions and jalapeños.

5. Far East Quesadilla $3.75
   Rice tortilla stuffed with imported Mexican cheese and exotic spices (ginger, pimento, and chives).

6. Juan Ton Soup $2.75
   A delicious blend of won tons with menude in an onion and garlic broth.

7. Imperial Fiesta Platter $10.99
   A sampler tray that is a buffet in itself. Features taster size portions of all of our menu items.

8. Chino niño Especial $4.99
   If you're not all that hungry or are under 12 this is the dish for you. Includes your choice of entree scaled to kiddie size plus a drink, our special tamarindo fortune cookies and an informative Chinese Mexican activity sheet.

9. Tamarindo Fortune Cookies $2.50
   Snackable fortune cookies with the baked in taste of tamarindo a house specialty and perennial favorite. An order comes complimentary with any meal, but why not take some home to enjoy at your leisure?

10. Pan Dulce Pork Buns $4.00
    Four sweetbread rolls loaded with succulent sweet and sour pork.

Thank You For Choosing
CHINAMEX

38. A description of the contents of a time capsule laid away during the heyday of the the Aztec civilization.

39. A love letter from an Anglo-American to an Afro-American before they are forced to elope.

40. Advice from a single mother to her daughter on how not to get pregnant.

41. An encyclopedia entry on the attitudes of native Hawaiians and native Alaskans on becoming the forty-ninth and fiftieth states in the United States.

42. A thank-you note to a doctor who saved your good friend's life.

43. The decision of a judge who decided to give your mother custody of your sister and your father custody of you.

44. A dictionary entry for each of *five* words that are not in your parents' vocabularies.

45. A list of the *ten* questions you feel adults never seem to be able to answer.

46. A list of the *ten* most important rules for the game of LIFE.

47. A top-secret report revealing the illiteracy of adults in the United States.

48. A menu for a restaurant that is frequented by winter slugs.

The Snail Without a Shell

111 Snail Trail Road
Invertebrate, Ca
95841

Appetizers -

Seaweed and Sponge Salad
    Lightly rotten seaweed and compost of the day all served on a bed of
decaying sea sponge. $ 4.50

Compost of the Day
    Our home grown week mix of kitchen seasonal fruit and vegetables.
                                                              $ 2.99

Apple Sauce
    Pureed, soft apples seasoned with your choice of wilted, seasonal flower.
                                                              $ 4.85

Pond Water
    Sun heated water with algae and recent topsoil run-off. Served with a side
of cultivated mold. $5.25

Moldy Day
    Moldy cheese served in a sauce of turned yogurt. $2.50
                        With moldy bread, add $1.50

Dinner

Fun Fungi
    Fresh mushrooms topped with our snail glaze. $10.00

Night Crawlers
    Dirt battered earthworms served on week old spinach. $7.99

Slug Surprise
  Skimmed pond scum, served with regurgitated tomatoes and stale crackers.
                                                $5.99

Spuds
  Locally grown rotten potatoes served with spoiled squash.
                                                $6.50

Deserts

Snail Berries
  Sun dried rotten raspberries topped with whipped snail slime.
                                                $4.89
Devil Cake
  Moldy angel food cake with rotten strawberries. $5.99

Sour Chocolate
  Chocolate moose made with curdled, sour milk. $3.99

Beverages

Beer: Non Alcoholic:
  Ladybug   Water
  Bugwiser   Sour Milk
  Lacewing   V8 tomato juice
  Redbug   LemoRaid*
                               Fresh squeezed Morning Dew

* Does not contain any snail/slug poisons.
** None of these dishes contain salt.

49. A survival guide to circus knife throwers and those being thrown at.

50. A sermon to your church on the rights of the wilderness and its animals.

51. The report of a TV weatherman who daily works in the Sahara Desert.

52. The shopping list from an upper-class matron to her hired help.

53. The words to a blind child that help describe what his blown bubbles look like.

54. A guide to help unhandicapped people relate to people who are handicapped.

55. The meeting of the East-West railroads at Promontory Point, Utah, from the point of view of a Chinese laborer.

56. An invitation to a cannibal's dinner when you are a member of a neighboring tribe.

57. A biography of a homeless man and his family whom you met on the streets.

Biography of Homeless Man

BY COURTNEY LAWRENCE

I met Yiprod while waiting outside one of those bath-rooms that you pay for. You put in a quarter and the door opens. Once you're inside, it warns you that it will auto-matically open after 20 minutes. As the door opened I saw a man with four cats, all sleeping on the floor of this public restroom. He asked if I minded not paying atten-tion to him while I did my "business." I, an upstanding southern girl, would have nothing of the sorts. Appalled, I went to push the button to open the door, but to my dismay it wouldn't open. The whole bathroom started throbbing and screaming "MALFUNCTION" at us. Here I was trapped in a public bathroom with a bum and his "family." Seconds felt like minutes and minutes felt like hours. Yiprod decided to pass the time by telling me his life story. He started out in life as a circus freak. Ev-ery day for the show he would glue on this fake snake-skin and become the amazing "Lizard Boy." He eventually fell in love with Bitty Jack, the girl who hosed him down after the shows, and they ran off together. They lived in the forest behind Bitt's biggest enemy, Sabrina's house. Yiprod and Bitty Jack filled their days terrorizing Sabrina. When she would leave to go shop-ping or for her daily run, they would sneak into her house and eat themselves silly. Sabrina, not being too bright, thought that the spirits of her parents were still in

continued

her house and she had to leave food for them to please them. So she did. They lived like this for years until Bitty felt she wanted a "real" life, "Where she would live in a two story house with a white picket fence, marry a doctor and have 2.5 kids," Yiprod told me sarcastically. She left him and he didn't know what to do with himself. He became a wanderer and eventually found himself here. In this bathroom, with me, STUCK! But this man's life was so interesting. I found myself almost not wanting to leave. I wanted to hear everything this man had to say. I picked up one of his cats, got comfortable and listened. . .

58. The terms of an early treaty between Geronimo and the United States government.

59. An application for admission to an embalmers school.

60. An advertisement for an all-violence cable TV network.

61. A complaint to a landlord about rats when you are an illegal immigrant.

62. A criticism of a movie that stereotypes Asian Americans.

63. An article titled "Touring Your Local Ghetto."

Touring Your Local Ghetto
BY MARBELLY TENORIO

In our local ghetto we see really nice houses but they're dirty with no lawn and graffiti all over them probably done by the same people who live there. We also have a convenience store at the corner with all the drunks and drug dealers standing in front whistling at every girl they see. Next comes the cars: all park in front of their homes sometimes looking better than the houses and owners; they rattle with crappy sound systems. We cannot miss the sirens of cops rounding the streets looking for some-body loud and rowdy to take in.

There's trash all over the place and garbage that hasn't been picked up in over two weeks. Most people are really proud of their ghetto but can't wait to get the hell out of there. But remember, you can take a person out of the ghetto, but you can't take the ghetto out of the person.

64. A State of the Union message from the first woman elected president of the United States.

65. A newspaper article describing the *ten* worst crimes against beauty.

66. What your résumé will be in the year 2006.

67. A song of praise to the Sun for keeping you warm and helping to keep life on Earth.

Song of Praise to the Sun

BY KRISTINE PEDRICK

The Mamma's and the Papa's wrote a song
About California Dreamin' all winter long
It's because their idea of fun
is basking and playing in the summer sun
Every time I drag my summer clothes out
from the back of the closet I give a shout
93 million miles from the earth
4.5 million years since its birth
Plants want to give the sun a kiss
For helping them out with photosynthesis
There wouldn't be oxygen in the air
without any plants to put it there
Without the sun's warmth we'd all freeze to death
Lungs would turn to ice with that last breath—
Now isn't that a depressing thought?
No wonder we love the sun a lot!

---

68. What your résumé would have been if you had been an Aztec priest.

69. An advertisement for a slave in a newspaper in Mississippi in 1840.

Slave Advertisement
BY DESTINY MOORE

SLAVES WANTED!!

New plantation owner with
young family just moved from Boston looking
for slave stock. Need two strong young female slaves
for house duties. Must be clean and healthy. Must also
be friendly and presentable. These will be in
my home and around my children
so must be able to trust them, no backtalk.
Also needed two male servants tall and strong
hefty boys for house
servants for cooking and odd jobs around the house.
They will also be around my wife and children
so must be clean and can talk.
Will need up to one dozen field hands, should
be young males aged 16–25, should have experience in
    fields
and know about cotton. Must be healthy and strong,
NO illnesses or disease. Also NO discipline problems.
Second generation slaves only!
I am willing to pay top price
for quality stock.
Contact Master Wills

70. A doctor's notes for his visits with a patient who is dying of AIDS.

71. The notes of a marriage counselor who has gotten a couple back together.

72. A brief textbook on how to rope like a cowboy.

73. A recommendation for Galileo as a teaching assistant in a college during his younger years.

74. A logbook of the man who discovered/invented plastic.

75. A Supreme Court decision that finds the actions of a particular racist congressman obscene.

76. The specific regulations against the production, distribution, and consumption of tobacco.

77. A mathematics chapter from a Mayan textbook.

78. The obituary for the man who invented the number zero.

79. A guidebook for horses on how to get along with flies.

80. Ten lines of graffiti that rhyme with the word *rhyme*.

Rhymin'

BY CASEY QUINN

Right now I'm gonna bust a rhyme
I'll kick back and recline,
With this bottle of fine wine:
Now I feel like I gotta spine
Cause I gave up droppin' a dime
Just to have a crack line
Drugs are no longer my shrine;
I got rid of my nine
Decided to try life, one last time
I started a business sellin' brine
Now I can say it's all mine.

Rhyme (rap version)

BY J. P. GREENE

Ten lines dat rhyme wit tuh werd rhyme
Lyrically usin that power of mah mind
I do it again time after time
One of a kind
Talent is hard to find
My style is wilder den two chix gettin drunk
off liquor and wine
I cause moe reactions den chemicals combined
My rhymes should be illegal some consider them a crime
Like a beam of light my rhymes shine
One, two skip to uh nine ten . . . and that's the end!

81. A description of the contents of a time capsule that explains the disappearance of the Mayans.

82. An interview with the man who invented speech.

83. An obituary for René Descartes.

84. The defense's argument for a commoner accused by the Spanish Inquisition.

85. A list of the breaches of etiquette committed by Captain Cook on the Hawaiian Islands.

86. A lesson plan on social studies by a teacher in the Dakota Territory in the 1840s.

87. A journal entry by Sacajawea on her first experience with Lewis and Clark.

88. A sermon in Birmingham, Alabama, in August 1956.

89. A "To Do" list by a female slave freed by the Emancipation Proclamation.

90. A butterfly's guide to avoiding deadly nets.

91. A yellow-pages advertisement for **Prejudiced People Anonymous.**

Prejudiced People Anonymous
BY KRISTINE PEDRICK

- Do you wait for the next elevator if a black person gets on before you?
- Do you refuse to be treated by a woman doctor?
- Do you believe that all Asians are bad drivers?

If so, you might be a Prejuholic . . .
Call for the location nearest you—
Affordable and Effective!
12 Easy Steps!
Recommended by four out of five prejudiced people.
1-800-Prg-Anon

---

92. A short history of aviation from the pelican's point of view.

93. A recipe for cooking possum during the Great Depression of the early 1930s in the United States.

94. A sexist doctor's guide to female patients.

95. A homophobic father's advice on dating to his son or daughter.

96. A boy's guide to dealing with anger *or* a girl's guide to dealing with anger.

97. Six slogans that could be used to help people stop drinking/smoking/taking drugs.

98. A weak person's guide on how to be assertive with salesmen.

99. A stressed person's guide on how to relax at work and avoid becoming a workaholic.

100. A child's prayer for saving the Innocent Earth.

101. A brief guide for women who are about to have mastectomies, including psychological and biological facts.

102. The analyzed results of a poll that attempted to discover the *ten* top reasons students hate homework. (E.g., do girls like it more than boys? Do juniors do it better than freshmen?)

103. A guide to understanding discrimination against members of the younger generation.

104. Give *three* specific examples of how differently you would be treated if you were a woman who was overweight and homely. If you are a man, give *three* examples of how differently you would be treated if you were weak and homely (or intelligent).

Off on a Tangent #1: Only Onomatopoeia

What is the sound made by two two-year-olds having a cottage cheese fight?

What is the sound a porcupine makes scratching his back against the bark of a tree?

What is the sound a water balloon makes when it lands on a cactus?

105. A woman's guide on how to choose a man who is right for her. (Or a man's guide on how to choose a woman who is right for him.)

106. Explain why you think that a man who is in charge can be "assertive" but a woman is called "bitchy." When and where do you think you first heard the difference?

107. Do you believe television gives children the wrong messages about outward appearances, sexuality, violence, beauty? If so, why do you think so? Do you know of any personal experiences to affirm your ideas?

108. Why do you think there appear to be two standards of justice in America: one for the poor and one for the rich and famous? Why is it hard to make a transition from one world to another—á la O. J. Simpson?

109. Can you describe a moment when you felt discriminated against for the way you were dressed? For your age?

110. Can you describe a moment when you felt uncomfortable talking to an elderly person because you weren't sure how much he or she could do or understand?

111. Have you ever found yourself raising your voice at strangers because you felt their understanding of English was unclear? Why do you think that happens?

112. What occasions in your life make you feel most stupid? Driving a car? Solving a math problem? Drawing a picture of a person? Not being able to sing on key? Speaking with an accent? Do you remember someone who made you feel self-conscious?

113. What *three* skills do you have that you are most proud of? How did you acquire them?

114. Can you describe *three* skills that you have learned from life and experiences that are not taught in school? Could they be taught? If so, how?

115. Have you heard of men or women who were successful in later life but were described in their childhood as "failures" or "lacking potential"? If you can, describe *three* of them and explain what you think was the turning point, what caused the change.

116. Do you have grandparents, relatives, or friends who have been happily married more than fifty years? Pick one couple—if you know them well—and describe how they relate to each other.

117. What would you like to be like as an old person? Would you like to retire and garden? Would you wish to travel? Would you like to learn something new? Would you like to care for grandchildren? Describe in 100 words how you would hope to spend your time in your 70s.

118. If you could not live in the United States, what country would you like to live in? Depending on the country, what *three* adjustments do you think you would need to make?

119. What advice would you give to a newcomer to the United States? Write a brief (250 words) survival manual that includes social, economic, political, religious, and educational practices.

120. What is your survival manual if you are a Native American in the United States of today?

121. Write your interviews with *three* different people living in Chicago's East Side considering their views of the space program.

122. Draw *three* rough drafts to be submitted for the final Aztec calendar.

123. Write a brief entry for a Mexican history textbook if the Americans had won the battle of the Alamo.

124. What 100 words are written in the textbooks for grammar school children about the end of the Vietnam War?

125. Write *three* journal entries for the man who invented glue.

126. What stereotypes of math teachers do you have that interfere with your learning math?

127. What is your idea of the listings in a telephone directory based on last names for a Sioux Indian reservation in South Dakota? List at least *thirty* names.

128. What would Nazis have written about Auschwitz and Dachau if Nazis had survived and won World War II?

129. Write *ten* lines of dialogue between a baboon and a gorilla on who is the ugliest. Include specific details and appropriate slang.

130. Which *three* regulations would you wish to see enforced to avoid oil spills on the high seas?

131. What are the motivations in the culture of poverty that cause people to join gangs, write graffiti, lose hope, and drop out? Describe *three* conditions that might make you feel like giving in.

132. Do you believe that "the love of money is the root of all evil" or as G. B. Shaw says, "the lack of money is the root of all evil"? What is the difference? Which do you agree with and why?

133. Write down the thoughts of the man who invented slippers on the morning the idea came to him.

134. Pick *three* TV advertisements at random that have women in them and describe the qualities of the women who are portrayed. Are these qualities that your mother or sisters have?

135. Pick *three* TV advertisements at random that have men in them and describe the qualities of the men who are portrayed. Are these qualities that your father or brothers have?

136. Make a list of *five* magazines you would expect to see in your own house or apartment when you are twenty-five. Why do you think they will be there?

137. Describe where you will be living ten years from now. Describe *five* possessions you will own that will have importance in your future history. What do they look like? Where did you get them? Why are they important?

138. America is frequently described as a culture that worships youth, a fact that means older people can be devalued. What practical measures can older and younger people take to overcome this obstacle between generations?

139. It is the year A.D. 2200. By international agreement, no nation can be invaded by a foreign power once it has proven it is civilized. Language is one such proof. Make a list of *twenty* words every American should know in order to prove America is civilized and should not be invaded.

140. Describe the case before the Supreme Court for which the following might be a ruling: Abortion is illegal on the basis of cruel and unusual punishment to the unborn child.

141. Write a brief advertisement (100 words) for an American product that would appear in a Japanese newspaper in Japan. What three or four qualities would it have that might appeal to the people and their culture?

142. If you wanted to introduce sumo wrestling as a spectator sport in the United States, how would you have to change it to appeal to American audiences? What *three* advertising slogans would you use?

143. People react to hot weather in different ways. How do you react to heat? Is it cultural, physiological, inherited? When you know it is going to be a hot day, what *three* techniques for coping do you use and how do you account for where they came from?

144. Debate topic: Resolved that NFL football is more cruel in the long term to its players than is bull-fighting to the bulls. Write out one good argument for each side of the issue.

145. Food is a cultural value as well as a means of survival. If you were hungry, list *five* things you would be doing without. If you felt you were starving, list *five* things you would be doing without.

146. Some people always get to places on time, others don't. Describe what kind of person is always late. Using details, describe what kind of person is always on time. What kind of person is always early?

147. Debate topic: Women carry purses, mirrors, eyeliner, lipstick, perfumes with them. Men don't. Therefore, women are more vain than men. Write one argument for each side.

148. Some people in high school and life learn in spite of dyslexia and dysphasia. Dyslexia means that a person's brain reverses visual signals; dysphasia means that a person's brain reverses and/or scrambles sounds. Sometimes such students are viewed by their peers as being stupid. Tests, however, indicate that such people are more often brighter than average. What *three* techniques would you use to compensate for these difficulties?

149. Why and how are frogs different from toads?

150. What considerations did Lewis have before he decided to explore with Clark? What considerations did Clark have before he decided to explore with Lewis?

151. Do you or does anyone you know suffer from asthma? Medical researchers believe the fatality rate worldwide is on the increase. What would you do—or have you done—to educate others on your condition or your friend's condition?

152. More than 400,000 people a year die from smoking in the United States. Medical evidence suggests these people are addicted. What parallels can you draw between pushers on the streets (of illegal drugs) and American tobacco companies?

153. It appears male dogs mark their territory by lifting their legs on nearby geography. Do male humans mark their countries and borders for similar reasons? Do males mark their territories—females—by impregnating them or conquer their territories by having sex with them? What similarities from this point of view do females have with things?

154. Did Jesus Christ ever tell a joke? If yes, what was it? If no, why not?

155. Many adults believe that children of their divorce suffer in only a minor way when they part ways. What friends do you know that can tell you if this is true or false? What aspects of their experience shows this to be true or untrue?

156. If you were sexually molested as a child, what kind of a person would you look for to trust with your experience? How long would it take till you could tell him or her? Why?

157. Many adults believe that sex and violence on television cause children to be more violent, more sexual. Other adults believe this is not so. Describe *three* movies that gave rise to sexual or violent impulses, and explain how or why they did or did not lead to actions.

158. History tells us that many creative people in the past who were great were also gay. Leonardo da Vinci, Alexander the Great, and Tchaikovsky, to mention a few, contributed to the greatness of their arts. Assuming it were a choice (it's not), would you be willing to be gay for your lifetime if it meant eternal fame? Explain what values are involved.

159. Some religions believe in previous lives. Assuming this might be so, what were you in your previous life and why?

160. If you were a slave in 1861 in the southern states and could be granted one wish, what would that wish be?

161. If you could see the future, and could talk to Anne Frank before her death, what would your conversation be?

162. A group of astronomers with advanced telescopes in the year 3000 have announced there is no life on any other planet. What is the first thing you feel and do?

163. If you could interview any famous person in history, who would it be, and what would your questions be?

164. If you were in charge of cloning people in the future as a part of a government project, who would you want to clone and why?

165. One of the problems of mankind in our world is overpopulation. Describe your legislation before the United Nations to solve this problem.

166. Your uncle is in a locked-down ward in an asylum. Your dead father has asked you to make a visit every so often. How do you prepare yourself emotionally for your first visit?

167. How do teachers make students feel dumb? Describe a teacher who made you feel dumb and a teacher who made you feel smart. What was the difference in the way they treated you?

168. A new student in your school is from China and is very timid and often picked on. You feel sympathy but don't know how to help. What do you do?

169. Your closest girlfriend has missed her period for three months, and you want to help her find out if she is pregnant. What do you need to be able to do?

170. Write out the argument you would have with your parents if they knew the next day you were going out to get a tattoo.

171. If you could uninvent one invention that bothers you the most, what would it be and why?

172. How would you describe men if men were strong in the ways women are strong? If women were strong in the ways men are strong?

173. Describe a teacher's classroom that made you want to come to class every day.

174. If you could ride one animal, would it be a camel, a horse, an elephant, or another? What advantages do you feel your choice would have over the others?

175. If you could be a fly on the wall when Mozart was composing, which of his pieces would you like to hear?

176. In what ways is your home life different from your school life?

177. If you are a child of divorce, do you feel yourself better or worse off, and in what ways?

178. Many parts of America once belonged to other countries or peoples. Alaska was called Seward's Folly. The Louisiana Purchase bought the Mississippi River Valley along with other things. Parts of Texas used to belong to Mexico. What country would you wish to buy to be a part of the United States and why?

179. Where would you be living if the Native Americans had won the war to keep the land to themselves and had put you on a reservation? What would your childhood be like?

180. You are growing up in America in the 1800s. Your farm is in New England. You have two brothers and two sisters. What are your morning chores?

181. Do some Japanese have racial prejudices? If so, what are they? How do you know?

182. Many people have heard the phrase (and film title) "White men can't jump." Is this a racist judgment, a stereotype, or a statement of fact? What is the difference?

183. Do you know how much money your father makes? If you do, how did you find out? If you don't, would you be willing to ask him? How would you do it?

184. If every time police came onto your campus had to be recorded, how many times a week would that be? Why don't public schools publish such records?

185. If you are living with your single mother, what chores do you do to make ends meet?

186. Do you have a friend who has told you that she has been raped? Were you able to stay friends afterward? Why or why not?

187. Do you remember when you first became concerned about issues larger than your own family and your own world (global warming, loss of the rain forest, racial discrimination, etc.)? What do you think caused it and what did you do?

188. If your son were the victim of abuse at school because he was small and unmuscular, what would you do within the school system to help him? What would you do to counsel him?

189. Your six-year-old son says, while watching a man clean autumn leaves off the main street, "Is he the janitor of autumn?" How would you express your compliment for his poetic expression?

190. If you are seventy and your husband is in poor health, without a will, what kind of verbal coaxing do you think would help him see the need for a will?

191. Write a short history of a homeless man or woman that answers the often-asked question, How did you get this way?

192. Write a short history of a prostitute man or woman that answers the often-asked question, How did you get this way?

193. Describe a situation in which you felt you were discriminated against because you were young.

194. Have you ever felt you would look better with breast implants? Describe how you would find out what you would need to know in order to make a wise decision one way or the other.

195. What *three* children's stories do you wish to be able to read to your own children and why?

196. Latex condoms can prevent diseases and unwanted pregnancies and yet are rarely advertised on television. Is this a form of censorship? Why?

197. Do you think your SAT scores made you feel good about yourself or bad? How did you come to understand what they are supposed to mean? Did a counselor tell you? Did anyone tell you what they can't measure?

198. What kind of a test do you think candidates for public office should have to pass? Give three or four examples of questions you would like included.

199. What words of explanation would you give to your son after he discovered you are taking a prescription medication for depression? And you have forbidden him from smoking marijuana . . .

Off on a Tangent #2: Imaginary Words

What does the word *cowclapper* mean?

What does the word *Noan* mean?

What does the word *Protogrunt* mean?

What does the word *recackle* mean?

What does the word *exghostify* mean?

Anonymous Student Answers:

"Skench" is the noun used to describe a person who is repeatedly sniffling and blowing his nose.

"Extramplee" is the word used to describe a defeated senatorial candidate who cheated his campaign workers out of their time and broke his country's bi-centennial trampoline.

"Monnle" is a type of pair of glasses that are de-signed to increase glare, blind the wearer, and there-fore give the wearer a reason for doing something stupid, such as hitting a parked dump truck, or los-ing points on his spelling test because he spelled his name wrong.

"Snuffledownagus" is an animal with eleven legs, a short tail, and a long trunk used to suck up cock-roaches. Using this trunk like a vacuum, the Snuffledownagus also blows out or down, any cock-roaches too big to fit into its mouth. This blowing down is the basis of its name.

200. Do you believe prescription medications should be advertised on television? Why or why not?

201. Do you want your husband or wife to be a virgin? Explain why or why not.

202. Most people understand the causes of the first civil war. If there were to be a second civil war, what would its primary causes be?

203. How did your great-grandfather die? Why do you know or not know?

204. Who was your most famous ancestor? What was she or he famous for?

205. How did your parents decide on your name? What were their considerations and alternatives? How do Chinese children get their names? Native Americans? Latinos? Muslims?

206. List *three* ways to protect the environment that have not yet been tried.

207. Do you think you can say how homework helps you learn? How would you describe the way it helps you learn and how is it different from the way you learn from your friends and family?

208. Would civilization be worse or better off if time were measured by a sundial? What arguments can you give?

209. What arguments are there for the idea that teenage pregnancies stem from the desire, like drugs, to escape from pain? What kind of pain could teenage mothers be escaping from?

210. Do you believe the statement "So many Americans are fat because so many non-Americans are starving" is accurate? What would body types be like if every nation had the appropriate food?

211. *Euphemisms* are used when a country or a culture finds some things too painful to discuss explicitly. "He passed away" means he died. "He's off his rocker" means he's insane. Make a list of *twenty* euphemisms and see if you can write why their antecedents are difficult to talk about.

212. Is tennis an upper-class sport? How can you tell? If so, what is NFL football? Why?

213. Write a haiku in French, Spanish, English, or German—or any other language you know well. Describe the problems you had in translating the meaning into your second language.

214. What is the smallest part of matter physicists know of? A meson, a quark, a positron? Describe what antimatter ought to look like.

215. What are the top *five* most dangerous breeds of dogs? Describe the process you used to find out. Why does the media focus on the danger of dogs?

216. Einstein once said, "Not everything that counts can be counted, and not everything that can be counted counts." What is it you think he meant?

217. Who is Don Quixote? Based on today's standards, would he be considered crazy or sane? By what standards would he be measured?

218. When Thoreau said, "Things are in the saddle and are riding mankind," what do you think he meant? What does his metaphor suggest?

219. What form of government do we have in the United States now? Democratic, plutocratic, oligarchic, republican, socialistic, dictatorial, or other? By what methods and definitions did you determine which?

220. What do you think the Bible says about materialism and greed? Can you answer this question without breaking the law prohibiting religion in public schools?

221. What form of self-defense would you prefer your own child learn? Tae kwon do, tai chi, kung fu, karate? How would you find out the advantages of each? Why?

222. What is a quinceañera? Why don't boys have them?

223. Many rap songs use the word *Nigga*. Does that reflect inherited prejudice that is finally accepted? What explanation can you give?

224. If the Ten Commandments had been twenty, what would numbers eleven through twenty have been for the 21st century? Why?

225. What high government figure was fired ostensibly for speaking about masturbation? Why?

226. What is your favorite book from childhood? What child would you ideally wish to read it to?

227. Why does it take more than 150 college credits to be a teacher and no credits at all to be a parent? Do they involve different kinds of learning?

228. Abraham Lincoln was a great wrestler. What kind of a wrestler do you think he was? Why do you think a president should have good athletic skills?

229. What do you think Michelangelo's graffiti would look like? Why was there no graffiti when he lived?

230. The divorce rate in parts of America is 50 percent. In arranged marriages, the divorce rate is 15 percent. How is this possible?

231. Would your dog or cat qualify as a morning dog or cat or evening dog or cat? What *five* characteristics would define either one?

232. How would society be affected if global warming required that heating was prohibited and Americans were forced to return to heavy clothing as a means of warmth?

233. Does science know if skunks smell to themselves as they smell to others? What research has been done regarding the olfactory senses of skunks?

234. What makes some mushrooms edible, some poisonous, and some hallucinogenic? Why do some religions accept drugs (peyote, etc.) and other religions do not?

235. Where do you think the idea that frogs cause warts came from? Why?

236. If alcohol, drugs, and music are each an escape from pain, is sex also? Why do you think so?

237. What are the sexual parts of plants? Where did they get their botanical names?

238. Maggots have been used recently and have been proven to cure infectious wounds when other medicines have failed. Write the dialogue between you and your doctor as you lie in a hospital bed with an infected wound.

239. How did wolves get the historically bad reputation they have?

240. If you were a plant on Earth, what plant would you be? Consider the qualities of different plants. Orchids are beautiful; bristlecone pines last thousands of years.

241. If you could save only *ten* species from the rapidly diminishing collection of endangered species, what would those species be and why?

242. Your girlfriend is pregnant. But you know she was with another boyfriend before you. Would you agree with her decision to have the child? How would you react?

243. What is the difference between safe risk taking and risky risk taking? Give an example of each.

244. Many people hate zoos. And yet zoos house some endangered species. If people were an endangered species, how would you want to be housed?

245. Americans are sometimes/often characterized as being ethnocentric. Why do you think this might be?

246. What foreign language poem would you like to be able to read and why?

247. Why are so few women writers in your literature text? Did women of the past not write? Were women writers discouraged or did they just lack the talent? What does your research show? Where did you get your research information?

248. How many women composers of great music were there? If you were a woman in the time of Mozart and wrote music, how would you get heard? How do you think fame was created in Mozart's era?

249. Who are your *three* heroes? What values do they embody?

250. How did the Supreme Court come into being? What decisions has it made that have been reversed? What in your personality suggests that you could have written a dissenting opinion?

251. When did sexual harassment laws come into being? When do you think they are fair and when do you think they are unfair?

252. America was founded by a revolution. Do you believe in revolutions? What kind? Why?

253. What is the difference between artwork and pornography? What is the Supreme Court's distinction?

254. In some European countries, women go topless on the beaches. In America, even a nursing breast makes people uncomfortable. Why is there a difference?

255. In your own bedroom, are there more pictures of your relatives or of pop stars? Does one indicate lower class and the other upper class? Why do you think so?

256. In high school America, most guys have sports heroes. Few talk freely of heroes like Einstein or Gandhi. Explain why.

257. How do we know our Sun isn't a part of another distant life-form's constellation? What would they call our constellation (in English)? Why?

258. What does the phrase "slave wages" mean? How did this oxymoron come into being?

259. Is the history of slavery in the Sudan in Africa similar to the history of slavery in the United States? How can you find out?

260. If a squirrel were bilingual, what other languages would he/she speak? Blue jay? Hawk? Other? Why?

261. If all Americans spoke three languages, why do you think their access to global information would be better?

262. Web "surfers" can learn how to make bombs on the Internet. Should the Internet be censored? How?

263. Everyone brings to learning and writing some baggage. Sometimes the baggage is in the form of past experiences with learning; sometimes it's what's going on at home or with other significant relationships (boyfriends or girlfriends). What baggage have you brought to your learning? Or writing?

Student Responses: Stories of Childhood
I
BY L.

Every day I got to school with thoughts in my head other than school. It has been that way ever since I was in elementary school. I have learned to depend on no one but myself. I am an only child and I live with my mother and family members from her side of the family. My father isn't around much, he only comes by to drop off a child support check of $150. That money is just enough money to help complete the payment for the rent. Sometimes he doesn't drop off the check on time and it stresses me out . . . a lot. On top of my father's irresponsible acts and his lack of encouragement for me to attend college, there is my mother who suffers from schizophrenia and paranoia.

Day after day I have had to and still have to deal with my mother's delusions and paranoia. Since I am her only child I am expected to stay by her side at all times, that includes sharing a room with her. My mother often thinks illogically and has delusions of persecution. There have been countless nights where I don't sleep, because of my mother's bizarre behavior, and have school the next morning.

My mother is also unable to hold down a steady job due to her illness. Since my mother is only able to work periodically I have had to work during most of my years in high school. All of my money has gone to pay off the rent and to fix my mom's car. My mom's car always

continued

breaks down. It either has a flat tire or there is something wrong with the engine.

When I'm at school I am constantly thinking of my mom. I get worried because my mom isn't supposed to be driving, especially under the condition she is in. There was a point in time when my mom and I couldn't afford a new tire for the car. Every time we would drive by a gas station we were forced to stop and put air in the tire. It was such a hassle just to get from one place to another. This was the way my mother and I got around for about four to five months.

Just recently my mom paged me during school hours and told me that she had gotten in a car accident. Apparently her brakes had gone out on her and she was unable to stop the car on time. She ended up crashing into another car. I couldn't stop thinking about how I should have been there with her, I was stressing out so much. I feel responsible for anything that happens to my mom. I felt so bad for not being with mom during the accident.

Family members also stress me out a lot too. When I'm at school I think about how much I don't want to go home to my family. Family . . . they always get on my case about my mother.

II

BY H. J.

My whole life has been hectic. Some parts more than others and only recently has it been getting better.

When I was born I had a heart problem. I had a hole between the two top chambers of my heart and blood

continued

was pumping back and forth between them, only releasing half of the blood to my body. So when I was four years old I had open heart surgery and I was one of the first kids to have an MRI. After the surgery, I recovered quickly and my metabolism speeded up. I became a very large kid instead of the tiny, scrawny, little kid that I was before my surgery. As school started I got teased a lot about my weight. I had friends but they still made fun of me. All through elementary school the same teasing went on. In the fifth grade I started going through puberty. I felt out of place and strange. It seemed that because of my heart surgery I was growing up a year too fast. I was the only girl in the fifth grade class with her period. I felt stupid.

In 6th grade (middle school) my mother had a nervous breakdown. She quit her job and started drinking. When she drank, her attitude changed and she started making fun of me. I became anorexic at the age of twelve. My mom started hitting me and punching me because I refused to eat, but at the same time, she wasn't eating either. She was using alcohol as a food supplement.

In the seventh grade my mom started blaming me for all of her problems. Everything I'd do became a petty argument even if I was doing something right. I quickly fell into a deep depression. Trying to handle life at home and trying to figure out who I am as a person, doesn't mix. I slipped away into a hole that someone else dug for me.

In the middle of seventh grade I became suicidal. One day before school started, I went into the girls bathroom

continued

and swallowed 450 Advil. Thanks to a friend who walked in 10 minutes later, she saw me and went and notified a teacher who called an ambulance. I was rushed to the hospital and my stomach was pumped. I stayed in a hospitalization program for people like me. I was one of 10 teens in the program but I was the youngest. I had therapy meetings every day and a Family meeting once a week. While I was there I started out in denial. I denied that I had a problem. But after about a week and a half I started to open up. In the month that I was there, I learned how to not keep everything inside. I learned to talk about my feelings. I was able to think about what my future might be. I thought about the people that I would have hurt if I had died. It's kept me going ever since.

In the 8th grade my mother's drinking habits and abuse didn't cease. Everything she did was my fault. At the time my sister was in 2nd grade. I needed to pick her up from school, help her with her homework, cook dinner, and get her to bed on time. While this was happening, my mother would be passed out, buying liquor, or yelling at me or beating me up. I began to take out all the pain I was feeling on myself. I'd cut my arms, legs, and stomach with a razor or burn myself. It relieved the pain inside by seeing the blood flow out. My dad is always at work. He works so hard to keep the house and pay the bills. But my mom spends it faster and faster. I once figured out that the money my mom spent on liquor was almost double what we paid towards our car each month.

My mom at this time has been in and out of 4 hospitalization programs and continues to drink.

continued

During my freshman year I made tons of new friends and I was feeling better even though I was still dealing with my mom. She was on seven medicines from Doctor's and she'd overdose or go "cold turkey" which has triggered seizures. But I was still feeling better.

As my birthday came around in March a few friends of mine (or so I thought they were my friends) came to visit me. I thought I was cool because I had two guy friends who were four years older than me, sleep over at my house. But by 11 pm I was pinned to the bed crying. I was being raped. I hated every minute of it and it happened just as I was feeling better about myself. When they were finished they held a knife to my throat and threatened to kill me if I said anything. I was so scared and so hurt that I just laid there crying.

The next morning when they left, I told my dad what had happened. He was ready to kill them. My mom was passed out on the couch with no care in the world. So we went to the police department and reported what had happened. The police found the guys and brought them in a few hours later. I pressed charges and they are still in jail. I will never forget that night. Since then I've opened up and helped people like me. I feel so much better about myself and I've made new friends. My mom hasn't been drinking for 2½ months and things are becoming somewhat normal again. But my mom does get cranky sometimes because she just went through surgery for a bleeding ulcer in her stomach. But that's OK. I'm 100 times better and wiser.

264. Who was Mother Teresa? What were her outstanding achievements? She was once quoted as saying, "There's a little Hitler in each one of us." Why do you think she said that?

265. Describe the history of how you came to speak the language you do.

266. "Language either keeps people prisoners, or frees them." How is this true or false in your community? If English were spoken only in the United States, what kind of conflicts could be reduced?

267. Do you think movies should be censored for bad language? What are the qualities of bad language?

268. According to some historical accounts, some Eskimo tribes have set adrift the feeble and the aged so they wouldn't be a burden on the group. What in American culture stands in the way of us doing this?

269. Some native tribes considered sharing their wives sexually with newcomers as a sign of friendship. How did this attempt at friendship depersonalize their wives?

270. What is the traditional way for the Tibetans to "bury" their dead? Why?

271. What language did Jesus speak? How do we know what he said? How can you find out what his written language looked like?

272. Why do older men seem to be attracted to very young women? Can you find evidence for male menopause or is it just a myth?

273. Can religions be included in the public schools without breaking the United States law regarding the separation of church and state? How could they be presented fairly?

274. What is it in springtime that a young hummingbird looks forward to?

275. What was your last experience in a doctor's office like? Did you feel comfortable and informed? Did you feel hurried? What would you have changed if you could have?

276. People do not always act rationally. When you have the flu, do you want friends to help you or to stay away? Why?

277. Interview a close relative over fifty years of age. Ask him or her what difficulties he/she encountered during his/her high school years and how, and if, he/she overcame them. Describe the differences between what your relative encountered and what you've encountered.

278. English is a very difficult language to learn. Why do you think it is used in many countries as a second language? Why did Esperanto not succeed?

279. Some people fear hospitals and doctors' offices. What is your theory about why this is?

280. In our culture, children play and adults work. When is this transition made? Why is there a difference? What happens to the children when they begin working too early?

281. Why do people listen to weather reports and traffic accidents early in the morning?

282. If you knew you were going to die, and could plan in advance the person(s) who would speak at your funeral, what would you want said by whom and why?

283. Why do you think Prohibition was a failure? How does this explain why the War on Drugs might be a failure? What parallels do you see?

284. In terms of taste in literature, what do you think your English teacher likes? Why?

285. How do you know when a dog is senile by his behavior?

286. When was the last time you truly felt self-hatred? What had you done or thought of doing that caused the self-hatred? When was the last time you felt simple and pure self-love?

287. Is there anything you wouldn't do for money? In order of priority, make a list of *ten* things you wouldn't do for money. Explain why you ranked them as you did.

288. What is the most beautiful thing in your life? Why are you attached so much to it?

289. Describe the *five* stages toward the complete love of another person or thing.

290. When you walk the beach to collect shells, what makes you bend down and pick one up?

291. Why did van Gogh cut off his ear? What do historical entries tell us?

292. What would be the first effect if your family ran out of electricity? Who would suffer the most? How would you make do?

293. Why are Chinese stereotyped as bad drivers? Why are Mexican Americans stereotyped as lazy? Why are blacks stereotyped as violent? Why are Jews stereotyped as greedy? Is it that what we see in ourselves, we see in others?

294. In many parts of the world, food is scarce and people eat what is available. Caterpillars, rats, snakes—all are parts of diets elsewhere. What is your top *five* list of uncommon foods you would eat—if you had to—based on their nourishment value (protein, etc.)?

295. Why did children in cold regions start making snowmen and not snowwomen?

296. Why do some people like to be scared by horror movies? What need is being fulfilled?

297. For what incumbent president would you be most likely to cheer, "Four fewer years!" Why?

298. Do you think the Chinese invented noodles? What does your research show? Who invented chow mein?

Off on a Tangent #3: Meanings and Metaphors

What does the metaphor "lovemaking" suggest?

What does the metaphor "the war on drugs" suggest?

What does the metaphor "sex drive" suggest?

What does the "war on poverty" suggest?

299. In 1999, one million babies were born to unmarried mothers. What happened to their fathers, statistically?

300. Why is the border between America and Canada virtually unprotected, and the border between Mexico and America guarded practically everywhere?

301. List *five* species that are monogamous and *five* species that are polygamous. Based on the criteria, in what category would you put mankind?

302. If your parents could give you an IQ test, would you want to know the results? Why? What do the different scales signify? For what purpose was the IQ test developed?

303. Interview a person over fifty years old, and ask him or her what phrases or expressions he or she no longer hears. Make a list of at least *ten.* What do they reflect? Often the phrase "That's more than I need to know" is heard. How much does one *need to know* between friends?

304. In your community, how can you identify members of the upper class? Middle class? And lower class? What are the status symbols?

305. What does the expression "The law punishes the rich and the poor alike for stealing a crust of bread" mean in terms of its paradox?

306. Why is it that people are told to call their elderly mother but not their father? Are there other examples where fathers seem devalued in American culture?

307. Who do you believe invented chopsticks? A man or a woman, a Chinese or a Japanese, and why wood? Who invented the fork? If research fails us, why? All the people on earth must eat.

308. For yourself, what is normal? How do you know when you're feeling normal? What are its characteristics?

Normal

BY BRIAN YOUNG

Normal is a concept I've fought internally forever.

What was normal did not exist to me. I was simple me. Not until I started watching TV and going to school did I become obsessed. One might say that American society was a catalyst for me wanting this "normal." I wanted to conform more than anything. To be like everyone else. To be thought of as everyone else, and to think of myself as everybody else. I did not know it yet but I was striving in vain. When I feel normal I feel nothing. Not good or bad, I'm just there. An emotion like happiness will take me away from the feeling of normal. I'll experience happy for a time till the feeling leaves. Then normal sets in. I guess it's like standby on a computer.

I thought (in fifth grade) that normal were the people on TV. Well-dressed, well-groomed affluent slightly tall people were my normal. Not thinking I had any of these made me angry at the way I appeared (kids fall into so many arbitrary-thinking traps). Life continued like that to fifth, sixth, seventh, and eighth, freshmen, sophomore and junior years. But during last summer I had a revelation.

At that time I had a great realization I was thinking Kung Fu and folding laundry. When it hit me I couldn't think of anything else for days. It was like a bomb destroying my inhibitions.

continued

> What is everyone going to do someday? . . . Die that's what. So I was to die and not matter anymore, making anything I did not matter. It sucked but was the truth which comforted me. I could stop worrying because life does not matter. This revelation helped me to understand me.

309. Who discovered the ozone layer and global warming? What are the current conflicting theories?

310. If Americans abandoned gas-fueled cars and chose to ride in electric cars, what would be the economic, social, and practical consequences?

311. Who was the greater composer of music for the piano, Mozart or Beethoven? If you don't know them, ask an adult who does. What answers did you get?

312. Many people have observed that mankind is the only species that sets out to kill its own kind. Is this true? Isn't it the only species that builds prisons for its own kind—human zoos?

313. If you could ride a Galapagos turtle, which sights in your yard would you slow down to see?

Galapagos Turtle
BY LAUREN SHAW

If I could ride a Galapagos Turtle I would slow down to see our pond because it is the most beautiful place in our garden. It sits underneath a gorgeous Japanese maple tree and gets just the right amount of shade so the temperature is always right. During really warm nights a lone tree frog croaks and completes the harmony with the crickets. The fish inside the pond are big and friendly because they are Koi and they shimmer beneath the water. The lily pads and frog moss aid in feeding the tadpoles that come in off the plants my parents get from the coast. I think the reason why I like this spot the most is because of the animals.

The second place I would slow down to see would be at the very top of the hill where I can look out over the entire Bay Area on a warm, clear night and the last row of grapes my dad planted bloom and smell like heaven (which is the best part of that spot). The grass is also the softest and greenest I have ever seen. But with all due respect to Mr. Galapagos Turtle, I don't think that we will need to slow down for anything, after all he is a turtle.

314. Some people borrow books and return them right away; others borrow them and have to be nagged to give them back. What is the difference in motivation and types of people?

315. What are *five* agreed-upon beliefs of Zen Buddhism?

316. Who were the *five* great athletes of the twentieth century? Who were the *five* great athletes of Rome in 100 B.C.? Why do we know other things about Rome but not about their athletes?

317. What would Leonardo da Vinci's résumé look like if he were shopping for a job in today's high-tech market?

318. What does "keeping kosher" mean? Do other religions have dietary restrictions? What are they and why?

319. Some few cultures practice *polyandry*. How would you adjust to this practice as a woman or man of the twenty-first century? What is the history of the practice?

320. How can there be a true *Survivor* show if there is always a cameraman there to help you in case of emergency? What would a real *Survivor* show be like?

321. Do TV shows/game shows invade a person's privacy/a couple's privacy? Why is personal privacy so greatly devalued and "fifteen minutes of fame" so greatly overvalued? Define your own idea of privacy.

322. Would you like to run a rare-book store? How could you make it interesting and profitable for you?

323. Would you like to be a wildlife guide or a fishing guide in Alaska? What parts of the job might be appealing to you?

324. Why does the news run frightening and horrifying stories night after night? Is its purpose to make you feel safe that the same events aren't happening to you? Noam Chomsky suggests that fear makes the populace easier to control. What do you think?

325. Make a list of the flowers you can identify by sight. Are any of them edible? Many tribes in New Guinea can identify hundreds that are healthful or harmful. What trees can you identify by sight?

326. What is the etymology of the word *god* from the proto-Indo-European? How did it come to be what it is? Describe the research necessary to find out. (Hint: Julius Pokorny)

327. What biological purpose can it serve that men are able to create semen over and over again, but women are born with relatively few eggs that age quickly? Why do women's eggs literally commit suicide (apoptosis) before they are born? (Hint: Natalie Angier)

328. Prometheus is given credit for having stolen fire from the gods. Could this myth have evolved from a chance meteor striking the Earth, which could have brought fire to primitive man?

329. Why do you think the Bible tells us Jesus was a carpenter? And not an architect?

330. What is the fear of open places called? What therapies are there for people with phobias? What evidence is there so far as to how people acquire them?

331. Why is it that no well-known animal evolved with three legs? We have quadrupeds and bipeds, but no tripeds. Does evolution favor even as opposed to odd?

332. What is the difference between koi and goldfish?

333. What is the difference between the Solar New Year and the Lunar New Year? How do celebrations for each differ?

334. Someone has described America as a country where "the adults are living in a PG-rated world and its teenagers are living in an X-rated world." What evidence, if any, do you see for this?

Youth and Adults

BY LESLIE SMALL

I think it's sad how utterly oblivious parents are to their teenagers nowadays. Parents don't talk to their kids anymore; how can they expect to know anything? A vast majority of parents are shocked and appalled of their adolescent's deviant ways.

Teens today live in a much more fast-paced, play it for keeps world than their parents grew up in. Especially in big cities the environment is corrupted by drug addiction and violence. Even if one isn't necessarily surrounding themselves with threatening individuals and such, it could come down to being in the wrong place at the wrong time.

Even in rural farmtowns teenagers are still exposed to something which could change their lives: sex hormones are raging and that component still remains when a portion of the city's dangers are removed. Another unerasable factor is the media.

I'm aware of the triteness of saying this, yet the impact which television has on our minds is profound. Increasing casual violence and heavy sexual innuendo situations not only color real life, but what comes through the dumb box as well. What the media portrays regurgitates into real life, yet we are able to regard the terrible things in life with our desensitized eyes and hearts. It saddens me to say so, but today's children live in a more hate-filled world.

335. Why are shooting stars called "shooting"? What are they shooting?

336. Why do neighbors have signs saying GUARD DOG ON DUTY? How does America's crime rate compare with other industrialized western nations?

337. Is Antarctica as large as it used to be? If it is a continent, how can it be smaller?

338. Many lives in America are without a sense of beauty. How can it be reintroduced into American homes? Where does a sense of beauty come from?

339. What issues were involved in the *Brown* v. *Board of Education* (Topeka) case before the Supreme Court? How have they been resolved today? Unresolved?

340. How do monks resolve conflicts in the Shaolin Monastery in China? How would you find out?

341. You are the captain of an oceangoing salmon boat. Where is your best location off American shores right now for a great catch? How do you know?

342. Why are there no "perfect storms" off the Pacific Coast?

343. While touring a botanical garden, you are asked to pick *five* of the most beautiful tropical plants there. What would they be?

344. The Mayan pyramids are similar to the Egyptian pyramids in some ways. What might those ways be?

345. History books tell us that when a dictator takes over a country, the first thing he wants to be able to do is control the media. Why would he want that?

346. What snakebite venom is the most toxic to humans, hemotoxin or neurotoxin? Why? What kind of toxin does a black widow spider have?

347. The practice of female genital mutilation is common in some countries, with millions of female victims annually. What is it intended to do? Why?

348. In the back of the dictionary is the abbreviation pIE (or PIE). What does it stand for? Why is it important to know the history of your language and how it is related to others? (See Calvert Watkins)

349. Why do so-called women's magazines and men's magazines both feature the same thing: partially clad women?

350. Is meditation a religious activity or not? Could it be taught in schools without violating the concept of the separation of church and state?

351. Why are some people good at giving directions and others not? What kind of intelligence is needed to give good directions?

352. What is the practical function of professional cheerleaders at professional football games? Don't people know *when* to cheer?

353. If you could never buy another Christmas, birthday, or Valentine gift but had to make them, where would you start and what would they be like?

354. Why were Roman numerals used to date movies?

355. Do you like to identify the footprints of wild animals? If it were a matter of survival where you live, what *ten* would you really want to know?

356. What do bears dream about when they hibernate? How long do they sleep?

357. What considerations does an Eskimo need to have in choosing the correct sled dog? What *five* names might he borrow from an Eskimo phone book?

358. "People watch movies these days because there's no time to read novels. Furthermore, you can watch movies in a group but you have to read alone." Do you agree with this analysis or not? How would you analyze the difference?

359. Where on Earth is your favorite natural wonder? A waterfall, a mountain, a sand dune? Describe it to a friend who has never seen it before.

360. What would happen if *all animals* on earth had to have mailing addresses? Not just domesticated ones like your dog and cat, but *all*, including the gopher in your front yard. What would the addresses be of those animals closest to you?

361. What is the disease you'd most like to see cured in the twenty-first century? Why is it important to you?

362. Would you rather live in the mountains or along the beach? Why do you think you chose as you did?

363. Are you a "morning person" or a "night person"? What is each person like? When did you first discover which one you were? What were your parents like? Do you think you could change your orientation if you tried?

364. What do you think Leonardo da Vinci's answer to global warming would be?

365. What country would you wish to visit that you have not visited before? Why?

366. Why do grown men play golf? Why are there so few black or Mexican American golfers? Do you know of any Jewish golfers?

367. Who is it who cleans up after brutal murders? Would you do the job for $250,000 a year? Why?

368. If humans had to live in cocoons for three months out of the year, what three months would you choose and why?

369. By the Emancipation Proclamation, your plantation's slaves have been freed. What do you make for your own rules of etiquette?

370. Who was the original Zorro? What does *zorro* mean in Spanish? What are the television stereotypes in the original series?

371. What is bipolar disorder? What is schizophrenia? What is depression? What is borderline personality disorder? Do other countries have these?

372. If dogs are pack animals, why do people leave them alone in apartments during the day?

373. If you were raped, who would be the first person you would feel comfortable telling? Would it be a woman or a man? Would you not tell at all? Why?

374. If K2, the mountain, is more difficult to climb, why is it that Mount Everest became a more famous ascent? Describe *three* famous climbs of either mountain.

375. Does the United States still have bounty hunters? Where do they get their job description? Write a short biography of a man or a woman applying for this job. What are his or her qualifications?

376. Until you are sixteen, high school is mandatory. Does this law assume that teenagers wouldn't want to go unless forced to? Why? Make a list of *ten* famous high school or college dropouts or uneducated people.

377. Who was Senator Eagleton? Where is he now? Why?

378. What is the day of a probation officer like? Of a truant officer? Describe the perfect person to do each of these jobs.

379. Some Native American tribes considered "counting coup" more important than killing the enemy. What was their thinking?

380. Why is it an important detail that the great detective Sherlock Holmes was a failure at playing the violin?

381. Do you think a researcher will cure the common cold? What will he/she be like?

382. Why do you think American comic books are full of superheroes (Superman, Batman, etc.)? Is the need the same as that which produced the Greek gods and goddesses?

383. Why is it that people don't get cancers in certain places? Cancer of the hair follicles? Of the earlobes? Of the fingernails?

384. Why do wolves howl? Is it possible to develop a language based on what they say? What is the difference between wolf-speak and coyote-speak?

385. Do certain races have a built-in tolerance to heat? If so, how do you know?

386. What are *three* highlights in the history of black witchcraft?

387. Do you think a snail and a slug communicate when they meet and pass each other? If they do, how do they do it?

388. If you owned a gun, what do you think you could kill with it? An ant? A skunk? A dog? A person breaking into your house? What do you think you couldn't kill with it? Explain why.

389. Do you have a friend with high SAT scores? How is he or she different from your other friends? Why do some colleges wish to drop the SAT results as a requirement for admission?

390. How would you explain to your eleven-year-old the meaning of déjà vu? What questions would he/she be likely to ask?

391. What is the difference between ravens and crows? How did you find out?

392. Why are physics and chemistry separate classes?

393. Many countries require their own language and two foreign languages to be taught in the seventh grade. Why don't we do that in the United States?

394. Why aren't funeral homes advertised on TV?

395. Based on his reputation, what kind of music do you think Sigmund Freud listened to? What does research tell you?

396. What are the advantages of listening to music over reading books? What are the advantages of reading books?

397. Where do monks go for a "fun time"?

398. What are the *five* most important rules of friendship?

399. Sharks have lived on Earth for millions of years. How is it they've survived so long? Would people be better off adopting their methods of survival? What could we learn from sharks?

400. If you could write an encyclopedia's description of one extinct species, what would it be and why?

401. You might have a friend who watches Bruce Willis movies, lives with his/her single mother, likes Led Zeppelin, and gets As in ceramics. What would you deduce about this person? Why?

402. What is the origin of the English word *fuck*? What etymological dictionary might include it? What words are forbidden in your household?

Off on a Tangent #4: Euphemisms We Love

What does "he went off the deep end" mean?

What does "burnt out" mean?

What does "peer pressure" mean? (Forced obedience and subservience from a weak person to a strong and mindless group of friends?)

What does "he went to meet his maker" mean?

403. Richard Ramirez, the "Night Stalker," a serial killer and rapist, attracted women groupies at his trial. Where can you get information to explain why this was?

404. In high school, you may have heard the term *sexual harassment*. Students can be expelled for sexual harassment. What is your understanding of the term in *your* school? In your school can girls be accused of sexual harassment by dressing provocatively?

405. What causes some people to talk in their sleep while others do not?

406. Do you believe intelligence is inherited? Which of your close friends is the most intelligent? How do you know?

407. What one song do you think you would want to sing if you were stranded on a desert isle? Why? Who would you want to sing it with?

408. I'm a Martian. What adjustments would I need to make for Earth's climate and terrain? How do you know?

409. What connotations does a path have that a street does not have?

410. Who is more intelligent: your mother or your father? Can you comfortably answer this question? Which one is more kind?

411. If state-mandated tests are good for high schools, why aren't there state-mandated tests for state universities?

412. Who is your favorite movie hero/heroine? What *three* admirable qualities does he or she have?

413. For what reasons might someone like old books better than new books? What qualities do old books have that new books don't have?

. If your relatives were to be put into a zoo, who would go where? Would your sister belong in the elephant pit or the gorilla cage? Give your assigned places for *three* relatives, and explain why you'd put them there.

Freud believed that the importance of work in adulthood was to find the original joy of childhood play. What does that mean? Is it possible in America in the twenty-first century?

Where is the Mona Lisa (La Gioconda) right now? How do you know?

If you were in a crash and had to eat human flesh to survive, would you explain it to the media or keep quiet? What would your considerations be?

Why are martial arts called "arts"? Can there be "art" in violence? What would the definition of arts be if they were all martial?

There did the word *devil* come from? What was its original meaning? How did you find out?

What are the ethical arguments against cloning human beings? Why aren't people as emotional about this issue as abortions? If you were a clone, would you be you, or would the other clone be you?

414. Why is it that Japanese generally have so little body hair? How is body hair used for drug testing? What was the original evolutionary purpose of underarm and pubic hair?

415. Why are constellations named with Latin, and not old-fashioned English names? Why not George the Comet? The constellation of Leviticus (biblical name)? Why are there no Christian-named constellations?

416. How did Alexander the Great get his epithet? If it were based on one quality alone, what would your epithet be? Why did people need epithets? What would some modern epithets be?

417. Can coyotes and dogs inter-breed? How can you find out?

418. What is the difference between a chrysalis and a cocoon? If you could be one or the other, and could make a change in the world, which would it be?

419. Investigation: Pick *three* teachers you know well and ask them what music they'd like to listen to in heaven—all the time—Beethoven, Bach, Mozart, or Brahms. Then ask why. Record your results.

420. If the Holy Grail were discovered and put up for auction, would it be against the law? Should it be? What law could be passed that would make it illegal to sell historical treasures? What other items should be included?

421. In old western movies, a black hat signified a bad guy, and a white hat signified a good guy. In America, black is chosen for a funeral; in China, white is chosen. Where does color symbolism come from?

422. What language is most closely related to English? Write down *five* words in that language and compare them to their English counterparts.

423. If women in the Armed Services were required to wear uniform lingerie, everyone the same style and color, would it violate constitutional law? What would the grounds be, since uniforms on the outside are accepted?

424. If you could have one pet (dog, parrot, snake, cat, etc.) for the rest of your life, what would it be and why?

425. What factor alone has allowed crocodiles to live for millions of years? How do you know? If survival is

the measure of intelligence, intelligent?

426. Suppose you could have only o love at first sight or a prearrang

427. What are the laws governing Census? Does the census fav one place for a long time?

428. Why do cats do nothing all selves, eat, and nap? Is it p ited memory remembers makes them tired without rhythm and do you think t

429. Why do some movie stars profile of what you imagi thinking.

430. In the United States, chi at ten and eleven years your own daughters and happening? How would

431. If your son or daughter or a cult, how could would you be able to t

439. In a bookstore, what aisle do you choose to go down first? Or do you just wander? Do you feel excited or bored? Why?

440. Legend has it that in the early decades of the twenty-first century, a band of upper-middle-class children formed the Robin Hood Brigade and robbed from the rich and gave to the poor. Did this happen? How could it have happened? What factors made it possible?

441. Legend has it that in the year 2008, the first woman was elected president of the United States. What do you think her first *five* bills before Congress were?

442. Are there any algebraic equations you can do by using leaves as integers? How? What leaves would work best?

443. It is said that a captain should go down with his ship. What useful purpose does that serve? Isn't all life holy? Doesn't the skipper have a family?

444. What values does the saying "You can't be too rich or too thin" teach young girls?

445. How many elements will be on the periodic table in the year 2500? What will some of them be called? What will the chemical symbols be?

446. Is it possible for a virus to breed with a bacterium?

447. Who suggested that exponents should be expressed up high and to the right of the number? Why?

448. What is Avogadro's number and why won't it ever change?

449. Paraphrase the following haiku:

imagined loneliness

disappears—

in the fog . . .

What does it suggest?

450. Why is it that mules are sterile?

451. Conventional wisdom has it that most marriages break up over small things rather than big things. Squeezing the toothpaste tube at the wrong end, snoring, etc. What *three* small things in a partner would annoy you the most?

452. Who created the quadratic formula? What was he/she like as a person?

453. Who were the last *four* winners of the Nobel Prize for economics? What were their theories?

454. Why isn't there a Nobel Prize for basketball? What would the rules have to be? How much money is involved?

455. Do you know anyone who should receive a Nobel Prize just for kindness and helpfulness alone? What has he or she done to deserve it?

456. Why isn't there a Nobel Prize for linguistics?

457. What is the real purpose of St. Patrick's Day? What is the history behind it?

458. Why do people refer to a person they have lived with and loved as "my ex"?

459. In your own community, which is more important: the racial barrier or the class barrier? How do you know?

460. How does an electron microscope work? Why is it hard to use in isolated areas where many difficult-to-detect viruses are present?

461. What does a phone call in the middle of the night mean to you? Some people fear such a call. How did this come about?

462. What does the Alaska Native Language Center do? How do you know?

463. How can Buddhists believe all life is holy? What about rattlesnakes and black widow spiders?

464. Describe the Human Genome Project. What information does it offer to the average citizen?

465. Exactly how rich is the current pope? Where did he get his money from?

466. Some teachers complain that students don't read or write as well as they did before. Is there any evidence for this?

467. Why do you think Einstein said, "Imagination is more important than knowledge"? What else did Einstein say about education and knowledge?

468. What are the warning signals of being overstressed? What connections have been made between stress and disease?

469. Why do most Christians worship the same time every Sunday instead of all through the week?

470. When was the guillotine outlawed in France? Why?

471. Who invented sign language for the deaf? Is it difficult or easy to learn? How is Native American sign language different?

472. Where did the Nazi swastika symbol come from and how do you know?

473. What does science currently know about pheromones? Could they be manipulated for commercial purposes?

474. What does the term *politically correct* really mean? Explain *five* examples of your own. Why is it necessary to have a term like politically correct?

475. Who invented the phrase "plausible deniability"? Why was it necessary?

476. How did the Tasmanian devil get its name?

477. Write a brief history of cannibalism. Include how old it is; where it came from; why it still exists.

478. Ex-President Ford's pardon of Ex-President Nixon is hotly debated. What are *three* pros and *three* cons?

479. Is it possible to have class warfare without racism? Is there a difference?

480. Who invented balloons? What was he/she doing at the time? What was his/her original plan for them?

481. What are the origins of the word *assassination*? Describe *three* failed assassination attempts and how they affected history. Describe three successful assassination attempts and explain how they may have affected history.

482. If you were given a nonnegotiable contract of one hundred million dollars and had to kill someone, who would it be? Why?

483. Select your *five* favorite songs. Which of the words within them do you wish you had written? Why?

484. If you could discover the cure to one disease, what would it be? How long would you be willing to work before discovering the cure?

485. What *five* thoughts from Pascal's *Pensees* do you think would most benefit the modern world? Explain how each one would help.

486. If you were a teenage girl and were considering a tatoo, what would you need to know? Who would you turn to for advice?

487. Many teenagers and adults are taking up martial arts to feel safe in the streets. What art do you think would be most effective for you and how would you find out? Should martial arts be taught in schools? How about weaponry?

488. From a dictionary of Shakespeare quotations, select *five* that are especially memorable to you. Why do you think they are memorable and meaningful?

489. Many Americans are overweight. If you were elected president, what plan would you promise to help them with? Who defines overweight?

490. If you could pick one drug that would make you feel better, and knew that you would not abuse it and that it wasn't harmful, what would it be? How would you get true information about it?

491. Some people love oceans more than mountains and others love mountains more than oceans. Describe how you would depict each kind of lover.

492. Since the oceans are not part of nations or continents, who decides who owns them? What oceans or seas belong to which countries? Does anyone own outer space?

493. Botanically speaking, how are roses and apple trees related?

494. If there is mad cow disease, why isn't there mad horse disease?

495. Violence in schools: Did it always exist? Are people just noticing, paying attention to it now? What part do better weapons play in violence?

496. Are rodeos cruel to animals? Are bullfights? How do these compare with the consumption of lamb or veal?

497. What did Abraham Lincoln's last will and testament give or say?

498. Many teenagers are killed every year in car crashes, etc. before they have a chance to make out a will. What would your will be if you had to make it out now?

499. How did the slug evolve without a shell (like a snail)? What is the advantage of sliding about unprotected?

500. Geologically speaking, would you rather be an igneous rock or a sedimentary rock? How do the personalities you would attach to each rock differ?

Off on a Tangent #5: Short Student Answers

Question: What events are in the World Series of Sewing?
Answers: "The hop, stitch, and jump," "the fifty yard hem," and "the 25 yard dart."

Question: What do you get when you cross Batman with Zorro?
Answer: "A vampire who bites Zs in the necks of his victims."

Question: How is the bear saddle used?
Answer: "For riding bare back."

Question: What part of the hummingbird actually does the flying?
Answer: "The wings, the humming is just for accompaniment."

501. St. Boeuve de Jeuner described Earth as "the center of stars and the end of stars." What do you think he meant by this phrase?

502. What *five* historical figures do you feel you could most trust and why?

503. "Dead metaphors" are those that are used so often we forget they are metaphors. A young fern is called a "fiddlehead" based on its resemblance to the head of a fiddle. "Uppers" and "downers" are comparisons to moods and pills. "What's up?" is even a kind of metaphor. List your favorite *ten* and explain why you like them.

504. If you could be either one, would you be an orthodontist or a proctologist? What *objective* factors (e.g., salary, working conditions, years of preparation) would you use to measure your decision?

505. If you were in an airplane crash over Canada, and could survive with the help of only one book, what would that book be? What other books teach survival in the wilderness?

506. Do you think it is true that homosexual pedophiles get more press than heterosexual pedophiles? Where can you gather evidence on such an issue?

507. Is it a myth that Asian American drivers are poor drivers? What research could you do that would find out if this were true or not? Whose help would you need?

508. What are the *five* most important steps/techniques in begging for a living?

509. Do you keep in touch with old friends when you promised you would? What happened that separated you from them?

510. What is the Madonna/whore complex for women? Is there an equivalent for men? Can you say that certain cultures promote it more than others?

511. If you were a homeless person, where would you try to stay? What is the difference between being homeless and camping out?

512. What is the difference between native trout and stocked trout and who could tell you the difference?

513. Where would you need to go to see a grizzly bear in the wilds?

514. What is necessary to get your taxidermist license? Would you be able to use it in another state?

515. If you could have autographed copies of your *three* favorite books, who would they be signed by? Why?

516. Goethe wrote; "Die Gegenwart ist eine machtige Gottin," which means something like "The present is a mighty god." How would this proverb be expressed in English? Is there a connection between it and Zen Buddhism?

517. Who would you want for your daughter's or son's ideal role model? What qualities does he or she have that you would like to have emulated?

518. An old Spanish proverb says, "Los montes ven, y las paredes oyen," which means something like "The mountains see and the walls hear." What proverb in English has the same meaning?

519. Write a short TV advertisement for an embalming school. What would the course titles be?

520. Why do some adults blame all teenage problems on peer pressure? What peer pressures do adults have?

521. Is a massage an upper-class privilege? What healing in other cultures is done by a laying on of the hands?

522. If you were a falling raindrop, what would your *three* wishes be?

523. If genetics permitted an octopus and a hippopotamus to breed, what traits/skills/capabilities would their offspring have?

524. Is creativity different from intelligence? In what ways? How were you able to find out?

525. How do you know if a frog is asleep or can dream? What dream might a frog have if he dreamt?

526. How could you count seconds on a sundial? Why are seconds important enough to be on every watch?

527. Do you believe in a real heaven and a real hell? How do you picture them in your mind?

528. Federal tax code allows deductions for the breast implants of "exotic dancers" but rarely allows deductions for what teachers buy for their own classes. What do you believe is the reason for this? How would you find out?

529. Is gossip necessary to bind people together? What is the function of storytelling (gossip) that may or may not be true? What animals would tell rumors if they could? Why?

530. An old Italian proverb states, "Dare in guardia la lattuga ai paperi," which means literally to "give the lettuce in order to keep the geese." Is there a proverb in English that means the same thing?

531. Who was Linus Pauling? How did he win two Nobel Prizes?

532. What medicines/drugs have the same effect on animals as they do on humans? Would horses get stoned if they ingested marijuana? How can you find out?

533. Why is it that *Playboy* and *Cosmopolitan* (among others) are printed on glossy paper? What would happen if they were printed on grainy paper?

534. What myth did early man have that would explain the rainbow? What would your myth be if you were early man?

535. What are the critical differences between man and beast? Is there any one thing special about mankind?

536. Why are a squid's eyes so large? How would a squid benefit in old age from eyeglasses?

537. Do cats get Alzheimer's? How does their behavior change?

538. Many societies have different ways of disposing of human bodies after death. In Egypt royalty was mummified. In Tibet, bodies are still cut into pieces and fed to the vultures circling overhead in the belief that the deceased's souls will rise quickly to heaven that way. In America, bodies are either buried (at sea or on land) or cremated.

If you knew you were going to die tomorrow, how would you like your body disposed of? Would you donate your useful organs to someone else/a hospital to help the living?

539. For many people, nightmares of spiders (or scorpions), being lost, falling, drowning, flying, being chased by monsters, being pursued by a criminal, and being in some other kind of danger are common. The troubling thing is that they feel as if they are real and create great fear as the person sleeps and as he/she awakes.

Describe the worst nightmare you've had recently.

540. For many children, the learning of the first swearword provides a sense of excitement at the idea of rebelling against what their parents think as proper. Other children feel a sense of being grown up, because, sometimes, swearing is what adults do. For others, swearing provides a way of releasing anger they have learned in their own environment.

Describe the circumstances in which you learned your first swear word. Who was it learned from? How was your way of saying it different from the way you first heard it said?

541. It is common for people to know that they are home by noticing certain landmarks. For some people, it is a familiar oak tree; for others, it is a street sign. For young children, it sometimes is a familiar tricycle, a rut in the road, a neighbor's dog, or an aging stop sign. For other people, it is the smell of their own house, or the sound of a turning doorknob.

When you have gone away from home and returned, what is the first thing you look for that means that you are "really home"? Describe that thing in no fewer than seventy-five words, including what it looks like, how far it is from home, and what it makes you feel like when you rediscover it.

542. Losing and giving up things is a part of life. Most everyone has lost a grandmother or a grandfather or lost friends by moving from one place to another. Sometimes the loss may be as insignificant as a lost favorite shirt or blouse; other times it may be as significant as a loss of faith or a good friend.

Describe a moment in your life when you were forced to accept the loss of a thing, a person, an idea, or a belief. Explain how you lost it and why you *had to* lose it. Describe the place where you were when you first you knew of the loss.

543. How would a return to riding on horses instead of in cars affect the environment, society, relationships, and people in general? What would you do better? Worse? What about drunken driving, auto insurance, smog, dating, romance, etc.?

544. What is the difference between excitement and happiness? Is one shorter lived than the other, or better than the other? Why?

545. Urban legends have become more popular because of the accessibility of email. They appeal to fears, hopes, doubts, etc. After examining *three* at the website listed in the appendix, write one of your own.

546. Where is the world's most valuable book? Could you find it on the World Wide Web? If not, why not?

547. Some people have psychiatrists for their pets. If you could afford it, would you have one? What would your pet be, and what problems might he or she have?

548. Some people suggest that Shakespeare was more than one person, or was some person other than Shakespeare. What are the arguments for this point of view? Where did you find them?

549. If the logic of reincarnation and karma is true, what must Leonardo da Vinci have been in his previous life?

550. Why do people have their tonsils taken out? What is the medical reason? What organs in humans are considered vestigial? In animals?

551. Many famous artists have been addicts, neurotics, or simply difficult people to get along with. Many have been Nobel Prize winners, some have been appreciated after they were dead, and some were simply misunderstood. Pick one of the following and explain what afflictions he/she had and what he/she did with it:

Emily Dickinson	Sigmund Freud
Robert Frost	Charles Darwin
Sylvia Plath	Charles Dickens
Robert Schumann	Yukio Mishima
Pyotor Tchaikovsky	Vincent van Gogh
Wolfgang Mozart	Pablo Picasso

552. If you had a teacher who admitted that he had spent a short time in prison for burglary, would you trust him? If you had a teacher who admitted that she was a recovering alcoholic, would you trust her? If your teacher admitted that he was gay, would you trust him? If your teacher admitted that she was a communist, would you trust her? In what order of trust would you rank these four, and why?

553. Is it possible that animals have consciences? Humans get a conscience from a sense of right and wrong, and thus feel guilt. Do dogs and cats and other animals get a sense of right and wrong? And thus a sense of guilt? What kind of guilt might animals have?

554. What are the *three* warning signals/symptoms to an oyster that it must make a pearl?

555. Mark Twain is quoted as saying, "Swearing provides a relief unknown even to prayer." Is swearing a necessary part of your life? How does it provide relief and when?

556. What single event in the history of the world would you like to celebrate if you could celebrate only one forever? How and why would you celebrate it?

557. What kind of people like to have goldfish for pets? What kind of people like to have shaggy dogs for pets? What kind of people like to have horses for pets? What kind of people like to have cats for pets? What kind of people like to have snakes for pets? What stereotypes of owners are there?

558. What is the current price for a hit man for organized crime? Who would know and could talk about it? The FBI? The NSA? The CIA?

559. Write *three* pages for days in the life of a monk who has vowed "poverty, chastity, and obedience."

560. What is the purpose of meteorologists on TV? What kind of education are they required to have? If it's a science, why are they so often wrong?

561. What *three* things do you imagine God worries most about? Or does God not worry?

562. Why are many fashion models addicted to tobacco and heroin?

563. There are designer bras worth ten or twenty thousand dollars. What is the purpose of such a bra? Are bras in general an adornment or a necessity? What do doctors know?

564. Who invented escalators and why? Do blind people find them user-friendly? Are they good for the physical condition of young people and health maintenance of older people? Why do we have elevators when everyone has legs? Where did you find your information?

565. Why are shark attacks front-page news when they happen about as often as lightning strikes that kill people? Do people enjoy savagery in the news and on TV? Why?

566. Are some women discriminated against because they are perceived as being beautiful? More likely to be treated favorably because of their physical attributes than their achievements in mind or soul? Are rich women prettier than poor women? Why do you think they are or are not? (Search: Cambridge Documentary Films)

567. Write a letter from an absentee hummingbird father to his young ones on *how* to fly very fast. Include what skills need to be learned.

568. The lion has been called "Lord of the Jungle." Why? Doesn't the lioness do most of the killing for food? Does that make her "Lord"?

569. Describe the kind of student who could get involved in the Annual Bird Call Contest. How and where could he/she learn the songs of birds?

570. What is the difference between wisdom and intelligence? What is the difference between creativity and intelligence?

To Rest Is "Silence"

BY NAOMI LEE

A Native-American once said, "If you cannot improve upon silence, don't try." Many try. Silence is something that is feared and encountered as little as possible. Truly, it can be a deadly curse. It is isolation. It is quiet. It is a mirror that forces you to look inward and face your inner demons. Silence can be a crystal summer morning; silence can also be the murky dangers of a winter's night. Silence is powerful, yet, in its very potency lies its strength. It confers strength upon those who are initiated and have undergone and understood the risks and blessings of being Silent. Silence is not for everyone. It is a painful and gut-wrenching process. If you make it through alive, however, Silence can never be taken away from you.

My parents knew the old saying that "children are seen but not heard," even though they came from Taiwan. My father worked to support my mother and me, so I was raised primarily by my mother. I learned Silence from her, and all the implications thereof. I was taught to behave, be obedient, be mannerly and above all, to be quiet. Loudness was not tolerated. Of course, a double standard operated. My mother was not bound by Silence. As she catalogued my innumerable, incurable, unbearable sins and shortcomings, I would be subject to stinging internal pain. It hurt, knowing that I was not and never would be good enough to meet her high standards. Thus, I learned to be a rock. A rock sits in

continued

Silence, lump-like. So I became a lump, and tried very hard not to show what I was feeling as I came under the antithesis of Silence from my mother. However, rocks have the privilege of lacking feelings. I didn't have the same privilege, so I cried, sometimes. Then I'd get double the wrath for breaking Silence and for sniveling. After hours of holding in sobs, I'd be allowed to leave my mother's sight. Behind closed doors I would rip off the head of my Barbie doll and throw the perfect waves of blond hair at my pillow. Then I'd put the head back on in preparation for the next time that I'd need to yank it off. This childish mutilation lost its appeal as I grew older, so I perfected the fine art of mentally cursing. Stepping outside of myself and away from my situation was part of Silence. Keeping still mentally and emotionally was another part. Learning to internalize my thoughts and feelings was a difficult lesson, but I learned it.

However, Silence is not without its blessings. I see things that others do not see. I hear things that others do not hear. I know things that others will never know.

Many try to break Silence, even when they can not compete with the eloquence in the absence of sound. I learned Silence from my mother, but now that I've passed the critical training period of childhood, the rules are more lax. Still, I find it easier to keep my thoughts inside. I see, rather than speak. I am Silent alone. I am not surrounded by the mindless chatter of those uncomfortable with Silence. My world is peopled with clouds and trees, raindrops and wind. It is lonely with these

continued

companions at times, but I stand strong. I do not regret knowing Silence. It is a quieting of the soul. It muffles a person's very being. But it is enduring, and after I am gone, Silence will remain. I can handle silence because I am unbreakable.

571. If you had to pick one movie that was a close biography of your life, what would that movie be, and why? What character would you identify with the most?

572. What sport will be in the world Olympics in the year 2500 that does not exist today? How will it reflect the culture and the values of the future?

573. You are a lab tester for the most ferocious animal on the planet. What tests do you devise? What are your notes for the top *three* animals?

574. What are mesons? Are they part of matter or antimatter? If a meson collided with a quark, what would happen? Who would know?

575. Does a pet cemetery reflect that a society cares too much about animals and not enough about human beings? Do most Americans desire luxuries, or necessities?

576. Which is more beautiful: a flamingo, a peacock, or a hummingbird? What traits in birds make one more beautiful than another? How would you rate a pelican?

577. If your world/life were built around one poem, what would that poem be? Why that one?

578. How do magazine advertisements sell images of female beauty?

579. If the greatest advice columnist in America is Dear Abby, who is Dear Juanita? What problems does she find most common? Who is Dear Miss Wong? What problems does she mostly face?

580. If your son or daughter got food poisoning in the school cafeteria, what actions would you take?

CONCLUSION

It is not difficult to see that writing prompts as provocative as some of these may cause some discomfort among students, teachers, parents, and administrators. It is my experience that writing can be a healing process in addition to being an expressive one. It is difficult to think of a great writer who has not kept a diary that in many ways rose above his individual pain and pleasure, even above his printed work, and transformed individual experience into a common human experience of verbal beauty. The fact is that some "answers" to these prompts should be kept confidential.

The more students respond to prompts such as these, the more likely they will be able to be free to find their own voice and their verbal bravery. Some of these prompts may be more demanding than the traditional five-paragraph essay in that they allow much more freedom of imagination. And freedom can be a scary thing.

Nevertheless, "writing to discover," as opposed to "parrot writing," must have its place in public schools. Parrot writing is that which does not surprise the teacher in content or form. On the contrary, writing to discover is that kind of expression that allows the writer to grow, to find what a grace the imagination is in problem solving.

APPENDIX:
COMPANION WEBSITES

This list of websites provides further information on topics covered by the prompts. I have listed them referencing first the corresponding prompt number to which they refer.

7. www.fbi.gov

8. http://www2.webpoint.com/azfamily_fitness/calcount.htm

10. http://www.lakhota.com/history.htm
http://www-personal.umich.edu/~jamarcus

16. http://aleph0.clarku.edu/huxley/CE2DarwObit.html
http://www.lucidcafe.com/library/96feb/darwin.html

17. http://etext.lib.virginia.edu/salem/witchcraft

25. http://www.math.sunysb.edu/~tony/birds

33. http://www.dannen.com/decision
http://www.csi.ad.jp/ABOMB

35. http://www.prolifeinfo.org

36. http://www.aids.org/index.html

38. http://www.indians.org/welker/aztec.htm

40. http://www.plannedparenthood.org/directory.html

41. http://www.hookele.com/kuhikui/ea.html
http://www.opihi.com/sovereignty
http://www.alaskool.org/projects/ancsa/ARTICLES
/ervin1976/Ervin_MuskOx.htm
http://www.akip.org/primer.html

44. http://world.std.com/~jimf/biking/slang.html

48. http://www.mertus.org/gardening/slugs.html

51. http://www.pbs.org/sahara/geography/climate1.htm

55. http://cprr.org/Museum/Chinese.html

58. http://odur.let.rug.n1/~usa/B/geronimo/geronixx.htm

59. http://www.nfda.org/resources/caregiving/embalm.html
http://www.wyfda.org/basics_3.html

67. http://www.bluehoney.org/SunWorship.htm
http://members.aol.com/zoticus/bathlib/helios

68. http://www.northcoast.com/~spdtom/a-god8.html

70. http://www.aids.org/index.html

72. http://www.juggling.org/books/lasso

73. http://es.rice.edu/ES/humsoc/Galileo

211. http://carmen.artsci.washington.edu/propaganda
/bland.htm
http://www.keepersoflists.org
http://www.topfive.com/arcs/t5101599.shtml

214. http://research.spinweb.com/news/antimatter.htm

217. http://milton.mse.jhu.edu:8006

218. http://libws66.lib.niu.edu/thoreau
http://www.walden.org/throreau/writings/default.asp

222. http://latino.sscnet.ucla.edu/research/folklore/quinceaneras

229. http://www.ibilio.org/wm/paint/auth/michelangelo

234. http://www.mushroomcouncil.com
http://www.matkurja.com/eng/country-info/food-drinks
/mushrooms/bad-ugly

238. http://www.augustachronicle.com/stories/072497
/tech_maggot.html
http://www.ucihs.uci.edu/path/sherman/order.htm

239. http://www.wolf.org/content.htm
http://www.pbs.org/wgbh/nova/wolves

256. http://www.gandhiinstitute.org

259. http://members.aol.com/casmasalc/newpage8.htm

264. http://www.ewtn.com/motherteresa/

270. http://www.lonelyplanet.com/theme/fatal_attractions
/fatal_sky.htm
http://www.tibet.ca/wtnarchive/1999/7/14_1.html

74. http://web.mit.edu/invent/www/inventorsA-H
/ baekeland.html
http://inventors.about.com/library/inventors/blplastic.htm

75. http://supct.law.cornell.edu/supct

76. http://www.cdc.gov/tobacco/overview/regulate.htm

77. http://www.michielb.nl/maya/math.html

78. http://www.andrews.edu/~dyoo/zero/zero.htm

79. http://www.ag.ohio-state.edu/~ohioline/hyg-fact/2000
2115.html

81. http://www.civilization.ca/membrs/civiliz/maya
/mminteng.html

83. http://www.maths.tcd.ie/pub/HistMath/People/Descartes
/RouseBall/RB_Descartes.html
http://es.rice.edu/ES/humsoc/Galileo/Catalog/Files
/descarts.html

84. http://www.internettrash.com/users/torquemada/aday.html
http://www.rraz.co.uk/alexs/python/MontyPython.htm

85. http://www.geocities.com/rcd113/cook.html
http://www.jetcity.com/~kirok/cook.shtml

86. http://www.sdhistory.org/ed%20fur21.html
http://www.amphilsoc.org/library/exhibits/treasures
/shindler.htm
http://www.indians.org/welker/cheyenne.htm

http://www.connerprairie.org/histon.html
http://www.geocities.com/herda.geo/sarahhfam1.htm
http://memory.loc.gov/ammeard97/ndfahtml
  /ngp_biblio.html
http://www.pbs.org/weta/thewest/events/1830_1840.htm
http://www.pe.net/~dtripp/biographies.Marvin.html

87. http://www.rootsweb.com/~nwa/sacajawea.html

88. http://www.abbeville.com/civilrights/chronology.asp
http://www.al.com/civil/timeline.html

90. http://www.npwrc.usgs.gov/resource/distr/lepid/bflyusa
  /bflyusa.htm

92. http://www.ecocanada.com/redberry/project/species.htm

93. http://www2.msstate.edu/~brb1/possum.html
http://elvis.neep.wisc.edu/~firmiss/mephitis-didelphis
  /opossum-recipe.html

99. http://www.uwec.edu/admin/counsel/pubs/cert.htm

101. http://umm.drkoop.com/conditions/ency/article
  /002919.htm

122. http://www.ai.mit.edu/people/montalvo/Hotlist/aztec.html
http://www.smith.edu/hsc/museum/ancient_inventions
  /hsc08b.htm

128. http://www.holocaust-history.org/dachau-gas-chambers
http://members.aol.com/zbdachau/index_e.htm
http://www.wsg-hist.uni-linz.ac.at/Auschwitz/HTML
  /Einfuhrung.html
http://carmen.artsci.washington.edu/propaganda/bland.htm

http://www.ccaccess.net/jmarcus/Archive
  /glory_of_war_euphemisms.htm
http://www.spectacle.org/695/ausch.html

130. http://www.epa.gov/oilspill
http://www.etcentre.org/spills

142. http://www.wnn.or.jp/wnn-tnyumon/beginner
  /nyumon.html

144. http://www.andalucia.com/bullfight/guide.htm
http://www.naturewatch.org/foundation/Bullfighting
  /bulls1.html

149. http://gto.ncsa.uiuc.edu/pingleto/herps/frogpx.html
http://www.cmnh.org/research/vertzoo/frogs
  /identification.html

150. http://www.pbs.org/weta/thewest/people/I_r/lewis.htm
http://www.lewis-clark.org/choice.htm

151. http://www.asthma.org/uk

160. http://www.liu.edu/cwis/cwp/library/aaslavry.htm

161. http://www.annefrank.nl
http://www.annefrank.com/index1.html

165. http://www.overpopulation.com/FAQ

169. http://www.plannedparenthood.org/library/FAQ's.html

180. http://www.mtholyoke.edu/marylyon/childhood.html

208. http://www.sundials.org/right.htm

271. http://www.library.cornell.edu/colldev/mideast/malul.htm

274. http://portalproductions.com/h/migrate.htm

282. http://www.fasterpastor.com/funerals/hearse.htm
http://www.geocities.com/Athens/Forum/6946/death
/funerals.html
http://www.arrangements.com/history/milfun.htm
http://www.japan-guide.com/e/e2060.html

291. http://www.ibilio.org/wm/paint/auth/gogh

293. http://www.balchinstitute.org/museum/comics/comics.html

317. http://www.mos.org/leonardo

339. http://www.watson.org/~lisa/blackhistor/early-civilrights
/brown.html

340. http://www.china-guide.com/qigong.html
http://www.travelchinaguide.com/attraction/henan
/luoyang/songshan_shaolin.htm
http://english.sohu.com/20010103/file
/1523,817,100030.html

341. http://www.cf.adfg.state.ak.us/cf_home.htm

342. http://www.usatoday.com/weather/whur12.htm

344. http://www.geocities.com/Area51/6683/pyr-amer.html
http://www.dragonridge.com/egypt/giza.htm

346. http://www.kingsnake.com/toxinology/menu.html
http://faculty.washington.edu/chudler/toxin1.html

347. http://www.fgmnetwork.org

348. http://www.bartleby.com/61/26/P0292650.html
http://www.yourdictionary.com/about/substantive.html

355. http://eduscapes.com/42explore/animaltracks.htm
http://wildnetafrica.co/za/wildlifestuff/juniorpage/spoor
/spoor.html

356. http://www.sciencenet.org.uk/database/Biology/0012
/b00800d.html
http://www.pa.msu.edu/sci_theatre/ask_st/021898.html
http://www.nature-net.com/bears/polar.html

357. http://www.sleddogcentral.com/canadian_eskimo.htm
http://www.matthewhenson.com/1913.htm
http://www.kabalarians.com/female/eskimo-f.htm

361. http://www.cdc.gov/nccdphp/major.htm

363. http://dubinserver.colorado.edu/prj/jph/index.html

369. http://www.nara.gov/exhall/featured-document/eman
/emanproc.html

370. http://home.earthlink.net/~rggsibiba/html/sib/sib6.html

371. http://www.pendulum.org

372. http://www.geocities.com/RainForest/Andes/4767
/social.htm
http://www.theatlantic.com/issues/99jul/9907dogs.htm

373. http://www.911rape.org/home/blank.hjml
http://ub-counseling.buffalo.edu/violenceoverview.shtml

374. http://www.peakware.com/encyclopedia/peaks/k2.htm
http://www.jerberyd.com/climbing/stories/k2

375. http://www.onworld.com/BHO/stories.html
http://www.wire.net.au/~melinda/bh.htm

377. http://school.discover.com/homeworkhelp/worldbook
/atozhistory/e/171250.html
http://www.slu.edu/pr/releases/120100.html

378. http://www.calmis.cahwnet.gov/file/occguide/proboff.htm
http://www.prospects.csu.ac.uk/student/cidd/occtable
/social/probat.htm
http://www.dashr.state.or.us/hrsd/class/6634/HTM

379. http://www.wwmag.net/Pages/coup.htm
http://www.ebookad.com/eb.php3?ebookid=9245

381. http://www.cf.ac.uk/biosi/associates/cold/home.html

384. http://www.pbs.org/wgbh/nova/wolves/howl.html
http://shade.grove.iup.edu/~wolf/whowl.htmlx
http://www.boomerwolf.com/verbal.htm

386. http://www.blackcrescent.com
http://www.witchvox.com/basics/wfaq.html
http://www.pitt.edu/~dash/witch.html

387. http://www.ipm.ucdavis.edu/PMG/PESTNOTES
/pn7427.html
http://ast.leeds.ac.uk/~agg/snails.html

391. http://sites.state.pa.us/PA_Exec/PGC/pubs/w_notes
/crows.htm
http://www.ange.fire.com/id/ravensknowledge

394. http://www.batesville.com/body_index_frames.htm
http://www.batesfuneralchapel.com/planning.html

395. http://users.rcn.com/brill/freudarc.html

396. http://www.mysteryinkonline.com/movies.htm
http://www.bookreporter.com/features
/books2movies.asp
http://www.hhpl.on.ca/library/hhpl/ra/MOVIES.htm

399. http://www.pbs.org/wgbh/nova/crocs
http://crocodilian.com

402. http://www.bartleby.com/61/95/F0349500.html
http://www.urbanlegends.com/language/etymology
/fuck/fuck_etymology_of.html
http://www.urbanlegends.com/language/etymology
/fuck/fuck/_references.html

403. http://www.crimelibrary.com/serials/what/what
social.htm
http://www.gmspider.com

406. http://www.theatlantic.com/issues/99feb/intel.htm
http://www.sigmaxi.org/amsci/articles/95articles
/Hunt-full.html

408. http://mars.jpl.nasa.gov
http://mars.jpl.nasa.gov/mgs/
http://pds.jpl.nasa.gov/planets/welcome/mars.htm

415. http://www.constellation-names.at
http://www.seds.org/Maps/Stars_en/Fig/const.html
http://www.emufarm.org/~cmbell/myth/myth.html

416. http://faz.macedonia.org/history/alexander.the
.great.html

417. http://www.cmnh.org/research/vertzoo/frogs/frogs.html

434. http://www.studiolo.org/Mona. MONALIST.htm
http://www.exploratorium.edu/exhibits/mona/mona.html
http://www.westnet.com/~rabaron/MONALINKS.htm.
http://www.studiolo.org/Mona/MONA37.htm
http://www.ibiblio.org/wm/paint/auth/vinci/joconde

436. http://www.alliancemartialarts.com

437. http://www.m-w.com/cgi-bin dictionary?book=
  Dictionary&va=devil
http://www.sacredspiral.com/Database/etymology
http://www.sacredspiral.com/Database/etymology
  /devil.html

438. http://people.msoe.edu/~tritt/sf/cloning.humans.html
http://www.family.org/cforum/citizenman/coverstory
  /a0001054.html
http://www.puaf.umd.edu/IPPP/Fall97Report/cloning.htm
http://users.compaqnet.be/jpnitya/science/clone.htm

445. http://www.webelements.com

446. http://www.microbe.org/microbes/virus_or_bacterium.asp
http://www.nih.gov/news/pr/may2001/niaid-07.htm
http://www.netdoctor.co.uk/health_advice/facts
  /virusbacteria.htm

447. http://www.thocp.net/sciences/logarithm_hist.htm
http://www.mathpages.com/rr/s8-01/8-01.htm

448. http://gemini.tntech.edu/~thurtsch/scihist/avogadro.htm

450. http://newton.dep.anl.gov/askasci/vet00/vet00004.htm
http://www.hamill.co.uk/british_mule_soc
  /gbmules.html

452. http://mathforum.org/dr.math/problems/cody.12.96.html

418. http://www.butterflyfarm.co.cr/farmer/glossary.htm
http://butterflygardens.com/bf-glossary.html

420. http://www.lib.rochester.edu/camelot/grlmenu.htm
http://www.bl.uk/exhibitions/mythical/grail.html
http://burns.tns.utk.edu/~jgriffin/grail.htm

421. http://www.colormatters.com/culturematters.html
http://www.browninglibrary.org/stglcolor.htm
http://www.projectcool.com/developer/gzone/color
/color_symbolism.html

422. http://www.towson.edu/~duncan/hellinks.html
http://www.nytimes.com/library/national/science
/020100sci-archaeo-language.html
http://www.santafe.edu/~johnson/articles.nostratic.html

425. http://www.pbs.org/wgbh/nova/crocs
http://crocodilian.com

427. http://www.pbs.org/newshour/bb/fedagencies/jan-june01
/census_03-01.html
http://www.rferl.org/nca/features/2000/03
/F.RU.000329112346.html
http://www.census.gov
http://www.census.gov/dmd/www/2khome.htm

428. http://www.mrs.umn.edu/~goh/Circadian/circadian.html
http://www.nhm.org/cats/biology.htm

432. http://www.mindspring.com/~zoonet/www_virtual_lib
/zoos.html

433. http://www.cfc.efc.ca/docs/00000983.htm
http://www.consciouschoice.com/culture
/havingfunyet1210.html

453. http://www.nobel.se/economics
http://almaz.com/nobel/economics/economics.html

460. http://www.mos.org/sln/sem/intro.html
http://www.uq.edu.au/nanoworld/images_1.html

462. http://www.uaf.edu/anlc
http://www.uaf.edu/anlc/index.html

463. http://indiaculture.net/talk/messages/65/158.html

464. http://www.ornl.gov/hgmis
http://www.ornl.gov/TechResources/Human_Genome/

466. http://www.fairtest.org/

467. http://www.aip.org/history/einstein/early2.htm
http://stripe.colorado.edu/~judy/einstein
/knowledge.html

468. http://www.mindtools.com/smpage.html
http://www.stress.org
http://www.anred.com/

470. http://www.cecut.org.mx/GALERIA/tortura/guillot.htm
http://pubweb.northwestern.edu/~erm638/project
/countries/france.html

471. http://inventors.about.com/library/inventors/bltty.htm
http://www.coloradomall.com/HTML/CULTURAL
/CULTURES/NATIVE_AMERICAN
/IndianSignLanguage.html
http://www.inquiry.net/outdoor/indian/sign_language
/top200.htm
http://www.inquiry.net/outdoor/indian/sign_language
/simplified.htm
http://www.deafblind.com/deafsign.html

473. http://www.sfn.org/briefings/pheromones.html
http://www.hhmi.org/senses/d/d230.htm
http://www.pheromones.com/

474. http://funnies.paco.to/ridingHood.html
http://www.jefflindsay.com/PCPhysics.shtml
http://www.re-quest.net/reading/rhymes

476. http://www.parks.tas.gov.au/wildlife/mammals/devil.html
http://www.parks.tas.gov.au/wildlife/mammals
/devil_faq.html

478. http://www.cnn.com/ALLPOLITICS/1997/gen/resources
/watergate/ford.speech.html
http://www.tompaine.com/history/1999/09/08
http://www.csmonitor.com/durable/2001/05/25/p11s1/htm

480. http://www.kfki.hu/~arthp.html/c/clodion/balloon.html

481. http://www.m-w.com/mw/textonly/lighter/shak/words.htm

485. http://www.ccel.org/p/pascal/pensees/pensees.htm

488. http://www.shakespeare-monologues.org
http://www.randyworld.com/shakespeare/billtop.html
http://members.aol.com/Jainster/Quotes
/william_shakespear_quotes.html

492. http://www.greenpeace.org/~oceans/news.html
http://www.state.gov/www.global/oes
http://www.audubon.org/campaign/lo

493. http://pages.prodigy.com/gardenshop/flwr22.htm
http://www.timelessroses.com

494. http://www.aphis.usda.gov/oa/bse
http://www.cdc.gov/ncidod/diseases/cjd/cjd.htm

495. http://www.nrahq.org/

496. http://www.hua.org/Bark/Rodeo.html
http://www.prorodeo.com/05.Animals
/0.animalWelfare.html
http://www.peta-online.org/mc/facts/fsent1.html

497. http://members.aol.com/RVSNorton/Lincoln2.html
http://www.netcolony.com/news/presidents/lincoln.html

498. http://www.ca-probate.com/wills.htm

499. http://www.ipm.ucdavis.edu/PMG/PESTNOTES
/pn7427.html

500. http://sln.fi.edu/fellows/fellow1/oct98/create
/igneous.htm
http://sln.fi.edu/fellows/fellow1/oct98/create
/sediment.htm

512. http://www.sw-center.org/swcbd/papers/trout.htm
http://www.nps.gov/noca/Trout2/trout1.htm
http://www.nps.gov/noca/Trout/trout1a.htm

513. http://home.att.net/~jrmusgrove
http://grizzly.sierraclub.org
http://www.canadianrockies.net/Grizzly

514. http://www.careers.co/nz/jobs/0b_lif/j80105x.htm
http://www.jobguide.thegoodguides.com.au
/jobdetails.cfm?jobid=640

519. http://www.wyfda.org/basics_3.html
http://www.melborponsti.com/scouts/songs/n
/nsong002.htm
http://www.nfda.org/pubs/june97

523. http://www.aqua.org/animals/species/procto.html
http://sailfish.exis.net/~spook/hipptxt.html
http://www.thebigzoo.com/Animals
/Hippopotamus.asp

524. http://members.ozemail.com.au/~caveman/Creative
/index2.html
http://www.quantumbooks.com/Creativity.html

525. www.sonic.net/~bigsnest/Pond/Lists/frognear.html
http://www.exploratorium.edu/frogs

531. http://ppi.orst.edu
http://gl0obetrotter.berkeley.edu/conversations/Pauling
/pauling1.html

534. http://www.zianet.com/rainbow/Relig.htm
http://www.enemies.com/html/oldtestament
/FLOOD_noah.html
http://haldjas.folklore.ee/folklore/vol6/rainbow.htm

536. http://seawifs.gsfc.nasa.gov/squid.html
http://seawifs.gsfc.nasa.gov/OCEAN_PLANET/HTML
/squid_links.html

538. http://www.organdonor.gov
http://www.organdonor.gov/signup1.html
http://www.shareyourlife.org
http://www.forestlawn.com/art/index.asp
http://www.seeing-stars.com/Buried2
/ForestLanGlendale.shtm

543. http://www.coxnews.com/newsservice/columnists/j_young
/06-02-00/YOUNGCOLUMN02COX.html

545. http://www.urbanlegends.com/ulz/index.html

546. http://news.bbc.co.uk/hi/english/uk/newsid_1035000
/1035014.stm
http://www.huntington.org/LibraryDiv/GutenbergPict.html
http://palimpsest.stanford.edu/waac/wn/wn06-1
/wn06-109.html

548. http://www.clark.net/pub/tross/ws.will.html

550. http://www.pedisurg.com/PtEducENT/tonsils.htm

554. http://members.ozemail.com.au/~dkgsoft/oyster
/oyster.html
http://www.mdsg.umd.edu/oysters/garden

560. http://www.jobguide.thegoodguides.com/au/text
/jobdetails.cfm?jobid=149

563. http://home.nycap.rr.com/useless/brassiere/bra.html

564. http://www.otis.com/aboutotis/elevatorsinfo
/0,1361,CLI1,00.html
http://encarta.msn.com/find/Concise.asp?ti=0362C000
http://www.india.schindler.com/ind/kgwebind.nsf/web
/Main-PassSafety-Users

565. www.flmnh.ufl.edu/fish/Sharks/ISAF/ISAF.htm

567. http://www.hummingbird.org

568. http://www.oaklandzoo.org/atoz/azlion.html
http://www.asiatic-lion.org/links.html

569. http://www.thewhistler.com/art_of_whistling.htm

570. http://www.cc.gatech.edu/aimosaic/faculty/kolodner
/creativity

574. http://physics.bu.edu/cc104/mesons_baryons.html

575. http://www.mycemetery.com/pet
http://www.petcem.com/famous_monuments.htm

578. http://www.about-face.org/

580. http://wellness.ucdavis.edu/safety_info/poison_prevention
/poison_book/food_poisoning.html